Self-Esteem and the Soul

John Monbourquette

Self-Esteem and the Soul
From Psychology to Spirituality

NOVALIS

© 2006 Novalis, Saint Paul University, Ottawa, Canada

Translated by: Bernadette Gasslein
Cover design: Caroline Galhidi, Pascale Turmel
Cover image: © EyeWire
Layout: Pascale Turmel

Business Office:

Novalis Publishing Inc.
10 Lower Spadina Ave. Suite 400
Toronto, ON
M5V 2Z2

Novalis Publishing Inc.
4475 Frontenac Street
Montreal, QC
H2H 2S2

Phone: 1-800-387-7164
Fax: 1-800-204-4140
E-mail: cservice@novalis-inc.com
www.novalis.ca

Library and Archives Canada Cataloguing in Publication

Monbourquette, Jean
    Self-esteem and the Soul : from psychology to spirituality /
John Monbourquette ; Bernadette Gasslein, translator.

Translation of: De l'estime de soi à l'estime du soi.
Includes bibliographical references.
ISBN 10 : 2-89507-567-0
ISBN 13 : 978-2-89507-567-7

    1. Self-esteem.   2. Self-esteem–Religious aspects–Christianity.
3. Self-realization–Religious aspects–Christianity.   4. Id (Psychology).
I. Gasslein, Bernadette II. Title.

BF697.5.S46M6613 2006   158.1   C2006-901222-9

Printed in Canada.

We acknowledge the financial support of the Government of Canada
through the Book Publishing Industry Development Program (BPIDP) for
our publishing activities.

NOVALIS   5   4   3   2   1   10   09   08   07   06

CONTENTS

ACKNOWLEDGMENTS

For the original French version of this book, I express my sincere gratitude to Father Jacques Croteau, who, despite having a visual handicap, agreed to review the text. I appreciate his perceptivity and insights. I would also like to thank Isabelle D'Aspremont Lynden and Chantal Beauvais, who read the manuscript and offered helpful comments. Much thanks goes to my longtime editor, Josée Latulippe, who prepared the text for publication, for her patience and precision.

Finally, I would like to thank Bernadette Gasslein, translator, and Anne Louise Mahoney, editor, for their skills in making this book accessible to English readers.

The act of entering into the mysteries of the soul,
without sentimentality or pessimism,
encourages life to blossom forth
according to its own designs
and with its own unpredictable beauty.

— THOMAS MOORE

These days we are inundated by books and articles on self-esteem. This modern panacea for all the ills of society is applied in areas as diverse as education, personal growth, psychotherapy, marketing, workplace relationships, spirituality, sports, and campaigns against delinquency and criminal activity, to name just a few. Almost every course and workshop in personal growth highlights self-esteem and self-confidence.

Many people today believe that self-esteem brings happiness and prosperity, at least in the short term.

A friend of mine who is a sociologist asked me one day how I explained this obsession with self-esteem. I offered a number of reasons for it — a return to individualism, lack of confidence in our current social systems, rapid social change, instability of institutions, people discovering their own resources and finding strength in affirming themselves, the worldwide popularity of the "American dream," the possibilities of entrepreneurship, the attraction of limitless fulfillment, the feeling of never being good enough — but none of my explanations satisfied me fully. One thing is certain: many people today believe that self-esteem brings happiness and prosperity, at least in the short term. (This current of thought on the importance of self-esteem comes to us from the United Sates, and in particular, from California, the mecca of the human potential movement. Europeans have been more cautious, fearing the spectre of excessive individualism, selfishness, navel-gazing, unbridled competition, and withdrawal from society.)

In this book
I examine the links
between self-esteem
and esteeming
the Self.

The findings of scientific studies and solutions from pop psychology have resulted in a range of definitions for self-esteem that are so varied, they sometimes seem contradictory.

SELF-ESTEEM AND THE SPIRITUAL SELF

An almost insurmountable barrier exists between psychological and spiritual growth, partly because of so-called scientific psychology, which developed in the context of the natural sciences. Like the natural sciences, scientific psychology looks for mathematical precision. It has distanced itself from spirituality, declaring that it is even opposed to religious institutions, which it deems too dogmatic.

In this book I examine the links between self-esteem and esteeming the Self. Through synthesizing psychology and spirituality, the book aims to give back to psychology its primary and most fundamental vocation: the study of the human soul. After all, this is the root of the word psychology: *psyche*, soul, and *logos*, knowledge.

I do not advocate the evolution of the spiritual self at the expense of psychological growth, or vice versa. Indeed, I am convinced that spiritual maturity requires a strong psychological self, and that the psychological growth of the Self is stunted if it is not based on the care of the soul and its spiritual resources.

THE CARE OF THE SOUL

Most books on self-esteem neglect the care of the soul. Because they do not know what the soul contributes to the construction of the Self, they overlook the resources of the spiritual self. To restore the equilibrium, I work with the spirituality of the Self found in the writings of the Swiss psychoanalyst Carl Jung. Jung defined the Self in terms of the *imago Dei*, the image of the divine found in the human person. (From the time of Descartes on, the dualistic conception of the human being, as a thinking substance stuck inside a body, prevailed. As a result, the richness of the term soul was lost and it fell out of favour. That is why I prefer to use the term Self rather than soul.)

The current popularity of spirituality influences scientific research, and contemporary psychological studies exhibit a renewed interest in the Self.

I present the methods and techniques that will enable you both to acquire a solid sense of self-esteem and to discover the Self.

DIFFERENT PATHS TOWARDS SELF-ESTEEM AND ESTEEMING THE SELF

In this book I present the methods and techniques that will enable you both to acquire a solid sense of self-esteem and to discover the Self. The path you will follow will depend on which area you are dealing with.

Self-esteem, built out of self-love and self-confidence, demands sustained efforts of understanding and will. The methods and techniques presented are inspired by different schools of psychotherapy, notably neurolinguistic programming.

Esteeming the Self, on the other hand, requires that we learn detachment and become able to welcome the symbolic messages of the unconscious. Instead of trying to love yourself and develop self-confidence, you must let yourself be loved by unconditional love and guided in the accomplishment of your mission. You must exercise active passivity.

People who want to both acquire self-esteem and learn to esteem the Self therefore face a double challenge.

CHRISTIAN FAITH AND THE SPIRITUALITY OF THE SELF

For the sake of those readers who are believers, I have included a final chapter showing the pertinence of a spirituality based on self-esteem and esteem of the Self to support Christian faith. Far from denying faith, the spirituality of the Self is meant to welcome faith. A faith that neglects the care of the soul will, in the long run, fail to nourish.

Part I

From self-esteem...

CHAPTER I

A brief history of self-esteem in the psychology movement

L et us begin by briefly examining the contributions of psychologists and philosophers to the topic of self-esteem; I will offer some assessments of my own along the way.

WILLIAM JAMES (1842–1910)

William James, the father of American psychology, defined self-esteem in his 1890 publication, *Principles of Psychology*: "The esteem we have for ourselves depends entirely on what we claim to be and do." James evaluated a person's self-esteem using their successes in relationship to their aspirations. In this perspective, the more someone was unable to fulfill their expectations of themselves, the more they experienced a sense of personal failure. In summary, to measure the degree of self-esteem of a subject, James confronted their success with their expectations. This is illustrated by the following ratio:

$$\frac{\text{reported successes}}{\text{expectations}}$$

James evaluated a person's self-esteem using their successes in relationship to their aspirations.

SIGMUND FREUD (1856–1942)

Sigmund Freud did not deal with self-esteem. Rather, he spoke of the ego being caught between the superego and the id. Constrained by the demands of the superego, whose inspiration came from parental principles, the ego was assaulted by instinctual forces. The conscious ego thus found itself in a precarious situation. Made fragile by pressures from the superego and the id, the ego was subjected to attacks of anxiety. The ego could only turn to defence mechanisms to protect it and relieve its anxiety.

Freud saw the unconscious as threatening and disorganized.

According to the Freudian dynamic, self-esteem scarcely has a chance to develop, because the ego is too busy defending itself. Any growth or flourishing of self-esteem is thus rendered impossible. Even more inimical to self-esteem is the absence of any spiritual authority that would provide the ego with stability and balance. Freud saw the unconscious as threatening and disorganized, like a volcano ready to invade the conscious ego with libidinal forces. Thus, for the founder of psychoanalysis, all spiritual, religious or artistic endeavours are nothing but the product of the symbol system of disguised instinctual forces, the effect of sublimation. This widespread, reductionist doctrine of spirituality greatly impoverishes the potential of the human psyche, and still today does terrible harm to the conception of self-esteem and esteeming of the Self.

ALFRED ADLER (1870–1937)

Alfred Adler placed the inferiority complex at the centre of his theory of the personality. He believed that from childhood on, human beings experience feelings of inferiority that last throughout their lives. To compensate for this sense of inferiority, people look for ways to develop a disproportionate sense of superiority. To the same degree that people feel inferior, they dream of being all-powerful and dominating. This theory is based on the concept of innate low self-esteem that the person strives to replace by over-esteeming the self.

Adlerian thought does not leave any room for appropriate self-esteem, which is a serious error. Those who would cultivate a profound sense of self-esteem, far from wanting to dominate or put down others, recognize their value and want to work with others without trying to compete with them.

CARL ROGERS (1902–1987)

Carl Rogers, the apostle of unconditional acceptance of clients in psychotherapy, recognized that most clients tend not to accept themselves as they are; indeed, they tend to denigrate themselves. He wrote: "In the great majority of cases, they hate themselves, and see themselves as stripped of all importance and unworthy of love." According to Rogers, unconditional acceptance of the client by the therapist would permit clients to learn to accept themselves as they are, and to love themselves, even with their weaknesses.

ABRAHAM MASLOW (1908–1970)

Abraham Maslow was one of the founders of the humanist school of American psychology that came to be known as "the third force" (the other two were psychoanalyis and behaviorism). Instead of studying people from the angle of mental illnesses, Maslow held – and the originality of his thought is revealed here – that it was important to be interested primarily in their mental and spiritual health. Consequently, he worked to identify the characteristics of those men and women who had reached their potential.

Maslow made a clear distinction between psychotherapy and the human potential movement. In his opinion, psychotherapy healed by addressing basic needs – that is, physical needs, needs for security and belonging to a community. The movement of self-realization, on the other hand, tried to address metaneeds related to fulfillment, personal growth, development of untapped potential, and creativity. In other words, it appealed to all the psychospiritual realities that come into play in the area of self-actualization. Far from being satisfied with the well-

Abraham Maslow worked to identify the characteristics of those men and women who had reached their potential.

15

Virginia Satir saw self-esteem as the heart of family therapy.

being or the better-being of people, the psychology of Maslow looks to their "more-being."

His most influential scientific contribution was to study the nature and conditions of peak experiences. Maslow was able to complete this research by asking those he studied the following question: "What have been the most wonderful experiences of your life?" He noted that people who had one or more peak experiences enjoyed a particular feeling of harmony and communion with the universe. From this observations he concluded that these experiences were indeed manifestations of the Self, not simply of the subjects' ego. In short, he highlighted the spontaneous spiritual revelations that came from the Self.

VIRGINIA SATIR (1916–1988)

Virginia Satir, from the communication school of Palo Alta, saw self-esteem as the heart of family therapy. As a member of the California Task Force to Promote Self-Esteem and Personal and Social Responsibility, she considered self-esteem in each member of a given family as an excellent criterion of mental health.

In fact, she argued that a family is dysfunctional when it does not allow its members to acquire good self-esteem and thus enjoy healthy autonomy. Her book *Peoplemaking* describes healthy family relationships in which self-esteem is recognized. She describes how, for example, in a given family, each person's freedom to express their emotions is a clear indicator of good self-esteem.

ERIC BERNE (1910–1970)

In his book *Games People Play*, the founder of transactional analysis, Eric Berne, describes in great detail the behaviours of educators (parents, teachers, and other key adults in a child's life) who were able to instill a high degree of self-esteem in the children in their care. He underlined the importance of signs of affection and attention in promoting in children strong self-esteem based in love and confidence.

Berne demonstrated clearly that a person who had poor self-esteem would tend to manipulate their surroundings by exaggerating their weakness or authority. On the other hand, someone who had strong self-esteem would not need to use social manipulation. These people show themselves to be authentic and honest; they know how to negotiate their needs in an adult-to-adult fashion.

Carl Jung was one of the first psychologists to make clear the organic relationships between psychology and spirituality.

CARL JUNG (1875–1961)

The place Carl Jung gives to esteeming the Self in his work is well known. He was, in fact, one of the first psychologists to make clear the organic relationships between psychology and spirituality. Unfortunately, the approaches taken by some Jungian authors since remain rather unsatisfactory, even misleading, giving way at times to unrefined conformity or linking psychology to spiritual concepts that are too ethereal or esoteric.

It is important to find a happy and accurate articulation between the psychology of self-esteem and the spiritual approach of the Self. This work of conciliation is made possible by the Jungian concept of the Self. As I mentioned earlier, Carl Jung defines the Self as the *imago Dei*. He made this the cornerstone of his psychology, which envisions enabling an individual to eventually become his- or her-Self.

Self-esteem left the framework of personal fulfillment and entered the world of American economics and politics.

THE CALIFORNIA TASK FORCE TO PROMOTE SELF-ESTEEM AND PERSONAL AND SOCIAL RESPONSIBILITY

In 1984, the Californian senator John Vasconcellos was named to head up the California Task Force to Promote Self-Esteem and Personal and Social Responsibility. The aim of this commission was to solve the problems that were on the rise among American youth, including delinquency, violence, truancy, poor school performance, drug use, unwanted pregnancies, and chronic unemployment. After three years of research, the commission concluded that formation in self-esteem cured these social ills. Self-esteem thus left the framework of personal fulfillment and entered the world of American economics and politics.

At the first meeting of California Self-Esteem in San José in February 1986, the idea of a National Council for Self-Esteem was born. This council expanded rapidly; its membership increased and many chapters were formed across the United States. In 1995, the National Council for Self-Esteem adopted the definitive name National Association for Self-Esteem (NASE).

Nathaniel Branden was the first speaker invited to the founding of the International Council for Self-Esteem in Oslo, Norway, in 1990. The objective of this association was to promote the consciousness of the benefits of healthy self-esteem and social responsibility. Forty-eight countries now belong to this association.

NATHANIEL BRANDEN

Nathaniel Branden is a pioneer in self-esteem. In the 1950s, at the very beginning of his career as a psychologist, he was interested in examining the harmful effects of the absence of self-esteem, such as anxiety, depression, poor school performance, low productivity in the workplace, fear of intimacy, alcohol and drug abuse, family violence, chronic passivity, and codependency. Self-esteem became the centre of his research and publications. His book The *Six Pillars of Self-Esteem*[1] is considered a classic on the subject.

I would like to make three remarks about his understanding of self-esteem and the means he proposes for acquiring it. The first concerns his definition of self-esteem. Branden defines it above all in terms of competence and aptitudes, not as a human characteristic. Thus he speaks "of confidence in our ability to think, of confidence in our ability to take up the basic challenges of life." Then he mentions the importance that needs to be given to our personal value, but always describes it in terms of personal success. In the same spirit he speaks "of the confidence to succeed and to be happy, of the feeling of our personal worth, of the power of affirming our needs and our wishes, of the possibility of fulfilling our values and enjoying the fruit of our efforts."[2]

Second, the technique he proposes for acquiring self-esteem consists of completing unfinished affirmations. This technique, which appeals heavily to the rational rather than to the affective side, leads to the doubtful outcome of good resolutions.

Third, Branden seems to reduce spirituality to a type of morality or purely humanistic ethic. He does not recognize the importance of making room for a kind of transcendence, not even that of the Self. The self described by Branden is stripped of any spiritual dimension. Cut off from its spiritual resources, this self is liable to fall prey to infatuation. Since it can no longer admit its misery, it believes it is all-powerful. Ultimately, this

Branden seems to reduce spirituality to a type of morality or purely humanistic ethic.

NLP builds on the conscious and unconscious resources of the person, and offers many ways of increasing self-esteem and self-confidence.

approach leads to a feeble self that deflates rapidly and becomes depressed when confronted by failure and loss.

NEUROLINGUISTIC PROGRAMMING (NLP): RICHARD BANDLER AND JOHN GRINDER

During the 1970s, a very promising school of thought, neurolinguistic programming, was born. Established in California by mathematician Richard Bandler and linguist John Grinder, its goal was to teach "excellence in outcomes." The two men developed the technique of modelling, which consisted of taking as models persons who had distinguished themselves by excellence in their respective fields: Virginia Satir, Milton Erickson, George Bateson, and others. In observing them, the creators of NLP unearthed the strategies that had enabled these people to attain such excellence, and presented the strategies that would guarantee immediate success. In short, NLP builds on the conscious and unconscious resources of the person, and offers many ways of increasing self-esteem and self-confidence.

ANTHONY ROBBINS

The work of Anthony Robbins, one of those exploring NLP, cannot be overlooked. His books *Unlimited Power: The New Science of Personal Achievement* (Simon & Schuster Adult Publishing Group, 1997) and *Awaken the Giant Within: How to Take Immediate Control of Your Mental, Emotional, Physical & Financial Destiny* (Simon & Schuster Adult Publishing Group, 1992) have been global bestsellers. As a dynamic speaker and popular writer, he has touched millions of people in many countries by his books, workshops, televised interviews, cassettes, and website www.AnthonyRobbins.com. Robbins has formed followers who spread his ideas on unlimited fulfillment for anyone who uses his methods. He has become the ultimate product of the human potential movement.

CONCLUSION

This brief look at the pioneers of the movement and the contemporary leaders in the field indicates that self-esteem is not a brainwave of modern psychology, but has been studied for over one hundred years. Self-esteem is a rich concept that is very promising for psychology as well as for spirituality.

Self-esteem is a rich concept that is very promising for psychology as well as for spirituality.

CHAPTER 2

Self-love and self-confidence

I am traveler and navigator.
And every day I discover a new continent
in the depths of my soul.

— KHALIL GIBRAN

PERCEPTION OF THE SELF

Perception of the self allows us to become conscious of different aspects of our personality: physical and psychological traits, moral qualities, needs, nature and resources, abilities and limitations, strengths and weaknesses.

My self-esteem depends on positive feedback from others and from myself.

So, if someone asked me to describe my current perception of myself, I would say, "I am a man; I exercise the function of priesthood; my career is that of a professor; I work hard at being a good communicator; while I'm a bit shy, I still like challenges." I recognize as my own the qualities that people who are close to me see in me. At the same time, I am not completely dependent on the positive feedback I receive from others. The more mature I become, the more I discover, through reflection and experience, other interesting qualities and aspects of myself. My self-esteem depends on positive feedback from others and from myself.

Consciousness of the self is thus at the origin of the affirming or demeaning judgments that people make about themselves and about their competences. Children are even more dependent on how others see them because very often they compare themselves with others in order to evaluate themselves. Little by little, as they gain autonomy, the esteem for their personal value and their competence comes from using themselves and their own progress as the standard of comparison. It is the sum of these judgments about ourselves that constitutes self-esteem.

The two forms of self-esteem ought to be valued equally. However, I would give priority to self-esteem of the person.

AN IMPORTANT DISTINCTION

Right from the start, I want to establish an important distinction between self-esteem for the person and self-esteem for one's competence. In the American context, two schools of thought exist side by side. One highlights self-esteem for the person him- or herself, considered as having a unique and infinite value. The other esteems the self for its competence.

Virginia Satir, who represents the first group, affirms: "I am myself. In the whole world there is no one else exactly like me." She insists that the uniqueness of the person be recognized and that all their physical traits, emotions, needs, faculties, qualities, and errors be recognized. Her act of faith in the inestimable value of the person relegates performance and output to second place.

Nathanial Branden, on the other hand, measures self-esteem by the development of abilities. His whole philosophy of self-esteem is contained in the definition he gives: "Self-esteem is the tendency to trust that one can respond to life's fundamental challenges and that one is worthy of happiness."[3] Branden emphasizes responsibility and output. Personal value and the respect due to the person occupy second place in his thought.

How can we reconcile these two tendencies – loving and accepting ourselves, or discovering our worth in our abilities and achievements? In my opinion, this is a false problem. The two forms of self-esteem ought to be valued equally. However, I would give priority to self-esteem of the person, according to the philosophical principle that action flows from being (*agere sequitur esse*).

SELF-ESTEEM OF THE PERSON

When we really love ourselves,
when we approve of and accept ourselves as we are,
everything in our life works.
It's as though little miracles spring up everywhere.

— LOUISE HAY

The very least we can do to recognize the right to life is to avoid endangering or degrading it.

Here are four signs of self-esteem for our being:

I. Recognize that I have the right to live

The affirmation of life is a spiritual act
by which human beings stop acting in a non-reflective way
and begin to revere their lives so that they can contemplate their true
worth.

— ALBERT SCHWEITZER

Normally we consider the right to life as self-evident, except in certain situations, such as when we are in mortal danger. Then the survival instinct takes over.

What about people who lose their desire, or even their will, to live because of their intense suffering? They must regain their will to live. How? First, they must ask for help; a number of different ways of controlling suffering exist. If suffering is lessened, they will likely decide to go on living, and to live well. A doctor told a mother who was distressed by her five-year-old daughter's depression, "It's good that you do everything possible to help her keep on living, but in the final analysis, she has to decide to live. No one can do it for her."

There are also subtle "suicides" that work against the will to live: smoking, drinking to excess or using drugs, speeding, and other risky behaviours. The very least we can do to recognize the right to life is to avoid endangering or degrading it.

*Being conscious
of our uniqueness
as persons means
recognizing that
our conscience is
inviolable; it means
living with quiet
confidence and
pride in ourselves.*

The convictions that sustain the desire and the right to life are the following:

- I have the right to exist;
- I am responsible for my existence;
- I am responsible for my whole body;
- I want to live, and to live in good physical condition;
- I do nothing to harm my health.

2. Be conscious of being unique

*The value of a man is measured
by the esteem in which he holds himself.*

— FRANÇOIS RABELAIS

Valuing ourselves as unique and irreplaceable persons does not mean believing that we are perfect or better than others. It does not make us compare ourselves to others, compete with them, or put them down. Rather, being conscious of our uniqueness as persons means recognizing that our conscience is inviolable; it means living with quiet confidence and pride in ourselves.

Unfortunately, some people doubt the value of their persons. They see themselves as worthless, undeserving of esteem and love, inherently defective. Others constantly compare themselves to others, an old habit that they learned as children from messages such as "Wow! Look at what your big sister did!" or "You're not as well-behaved as your cousin" or "You don't work as hard as the others." Each child, each person is unique; comparisons are inappropriate. Max Ehrmann said, "If you compare yourself to others, you can become proud and bitter, because there will always be people who are better than you and others worse than you."

To counteract these negative messages, it is important to reinforce people's convictions about their value and uniqueness:

- I am valuable;
- I am unique in the world; there is no one else like me;
- I am very important;
- I respect myself and I expect others to respect me;
- I have personal dignity;
- I feel that I am worthy of appreciation;
- I am proud of myself;
- I am the best witness of what I'm like on the inside (of what I see, hear, and feel there).

Learning to accept all the aspects of ourselves as part of our personality is a major challenge for self-esteem.

3. Accept all aspects of the person

Because I recognize as mine everything that belongs to me,
I can know myself better.
By doing this, I can love myself
and have a good relationship with each part of myself.

— VIRGINIA SATIR

Learning to accept all the aspects of ourselves — our body; our different, fluctuating emotions, thoughts, desires, dreams; and even our shadow — as part of our personality is a major challenge for self-esteem. Ideally, we would allow conscious and unconscious material to emerge in ourselves without questioning, rationalizing, expressing or being conscious of it. But instead we tend to block an unpleasant feeling, a sense of being ill-at-ease, an embarrassing emotion, a bothersome thought, an indecent desire or a crazy dream. We're ready to avoid them, hide them, push them down as unacceptable. But these approaches only fill up our shadow side (see pages 140–149 on the development of the shadow in the personality). What we don't want

Love of self begins with authentic compassion towards the self.

to recognize and accept continues to work in us and on us, even when we repress it.

Instead of repressing this material, we need to become observers of it. Rather than identifying ourselves with every passing state of mind and heart, we let them go by, as if they are so many passing clouds. This is the purpose and effect of authentic meditation.

People who welcome all the different aspects of their being will let themselves be guided by the following convictions:

- I will try on all parts of my being just because they are mine;
- I accept the presence of my thoughts, even if I can't always act on them;
- I will feel my emotions and feelings even if they are painful or frustrating;
- I will try to live in harmony with all aspects of my being.

4. See myself as loved, and loving myself

The worst solitude is not to be alone,
but to be an unbearable companion for oneself.
The most violent solitude is to be bored with one's own company.

— JACQUES SALOME

When family members and teachers freely lavish attention and affection on children, children learn to treat themselves warmly and kindly. From this they grow to see themselves as their own best friend, listening to, understanding, encouraging, and expressing kind and compassionate love towards themselves.

Love of self begins with authentic compassion towards the self. People who love themselves don't fight with themselves about mistakes they've made, blame themselves when they're suffering or humiliate themselves when they have failed. Instead, they listen to, console, encourage, and trust themselves.

We cannot love others if we do not love ourselves.

Such faithful and constant love of self also plays a determining role in love of neighbour. We cannot love others if we do not love ourselves.

Love of self rests on the following convictions:
- I am sure that I am loved and lovable;
- I am compassionate towards myself;
- I forgive my errors and faults;
- I am my own best friend;
- I speak to myself tenderly;
- I encourage myself in difficult times.

SELF-ESTEEM FOR OUR ABILITIES

The second form of self-esteem has to do with our competence: our confidence in our abilities, willingness to master tasks, and determination to accomplish projects and fulfill dreams. It has nothing to do with the feeling of being all-powerful and all-knowing.

This type of self-esteem enables us to believe in our ability to understand, to carry out our work and to respond to the ongoing challenges of life.

Here are the indicators of this kind of self-esteem and its underlying convictions.

1. Believing in our ability to learn

Many people do not believe that they can learn. They doubt themselves, thinking that they are less intelligent than others, that they have to work harder than others to succeed, that they have to learn everything by heart, for example. People

29

Recognizing our aptitudes and limits and refusing to compare ourselves to others are two essential conditions for gaining an appropriate sense of self-esteem in terms of competence.

like this are following the limits imposed by misguided parents or teachers who discouraged them constantly and made them doubt their abilities.

In contrast, people who have strong self-esteem trust their mental faculties: their intelligence, imagination, judgment, ability to learn in logical way. For example, I know a man who learned to use a computer at the age of 82. Not only has he mastered word processing, but he also reproduces his sketches and paintings so he can improve them.

Such people nourish in themselves a certitude and assurance that increases their ability to learn. They cherish the following beliefs:

- I am gifted with intellectual abilities;
- I am confident of my ability to undertake ordinary tasks and to shoulder life's daily challenges;
- I set realistic objectives for myself and know how to accomplish them.

2. Accepting our own levels of competence without comparing ourselves to others

Recognizing our aptitudes and limits and refusing to compare ourselves to others are two essential conditions for gaining an appropriate sense of self-esteem in terms of competence.

We must of course be realistic about these aptitudes and limits so we can grow. If we set the bar too high, we become discouraged or paralyzed. This happened to me when I was writing my doctoral thesis. I told myself, "I have to write ten pages per day." At the end of the day, when I had not been able to finish a single page, I became frustrated, anxious, and depressed. When I stopped forcing myself to do the impossible, I learned to be satisfied with the amount I had accomplished, however small.

These small gains were worth more than lofty expectations that I couldn't meet.

People who trust themselves overcome their fear of risk-taking. They are not haunted by the possibility of making a mistake. If they do make mistakes, they know how to repair them; they consider them opportunities for learning what to avoid.

This trust is nourished by the following beliefs:

- I feel I am capable;
- I don't need to compare myself to others;
- I compare my current achievements with my past ones;
- I accept my current level of competence, even as I strive to improve;
- I dare to try new challenges;
- I transform my mistakes into sources of information for what I shouldn't do;
- I am sure I can complete my projects.

Those who value themselves appropriately remember their former successes and take comfort in them.

3. Knowing how to value ourselves after every success, no matter how small

Success breeds success. Those who value themselves appropriately remember their former successes and take comfort in them. They constantly live in the hope of succeeding again. These people look to the future with optimism. They don't doubt their own potential for success: they see and feel themselves being successful, and tell themselves so. This vision gives them momentum and hope. Rather than being discouraged by the thought of any obstacles and difficulties that they will encounter, these challenges motivate them. They have come to know that they can overcome these obstacles, thanks to their own resourcefulness and others' support.

The convictions that underpin this kind of self-esteem are the following:

31

The ultimate level of self-confidence consists in fulfilling our personal mission.

- I feel encouraged by small successes;
- I set realistic objectives for myself;
- I congratulate myself on my successes;
- I see myself as succeeding;
- I have learned to overcome obstacles.

4. Seeking our mission and fulfilling it

The ultimate level of self-confidence consists in fulfilling our personal mission. Our mission is much bigger than having a job or a comfortable career. It responds to the "dream of our soul," to a deep yearning of the heart to serve the community. Transcending the ambitions of the ego, it is located instead in the stirrings of the Self. But be careful! If we do not enjoy great self-esteem for our competence and a strong sense of self-confidence, it is highly unlikely that we will risk following our personal mission.

Once we have discovered the "dream of our soul" and acquired the conviction that we can attain it no matter what sacrifices it demands, we will have reached a state of true fulfillment. Those who have the courage to follow the passion of their heart will feel alive and creative in serving society.

To sustain this passion as they look to fulfill this mission, people must nourish these convictions:

- I am convinced that I have a personal mission;
- I look for it in what I am most passionate and enthused about;
- I will be faithful to it despite obstacles and opposition from the people around me;
- I am conscious right now of having a unique vocation and of being able to fulfill my role of co-creator of the universe.

CONCLUSION

If esteem for ourselves and esteem for our abilities are unbalanced, we will not act in healthy ways. Those who have high self-esteem for themselves as a person, but lack confidence in their abilities, tend not to follow through on their responsibilities and will avoid taking risks. Moreover, they may insist on being accepted despite their inadequacies and passivity. They will socialize madly to make sure people forget their lack of initiative and their laziness. They may pretend that their niceness and attractiveness excuse them from carrying out ordinary tasks or responsibilities. They specialize in seduction and excuses, manipulating others to wait on them.

On the other hand, those who have developed their talents to the maximum, but have no personal self-esteem – workaholics, perfectionists, perfect rescuers, the fanatically dutiful – are equally unhealthy. Their work and their devotion get them a lot of attention, but this will not lead to the love they seek. Even during their best performances, they will have the feeling of being false and they will suffer the secret anguish of not being loved. One young woman I met refused to use her many talents out of fear that she would be valued only for her competence. Her lack of self-esteem for her person made her sabotage her many talents to avoid being exploited.

It is not unusual to meet people who are conscious of being enslaved by their career or their profession. Particularly at midlife, they wake up to the fact that they don't love themselves and are not loved. This awakening often leaves them depressed and makes them discount the value of the very gifts that were their claim to fame.

If esteem for ourselves and esteem for our abilities are unbalanced, we will not act in healthy ways.

Both types of self-esteem — for both the person and for competence — are necessary. The key is to find the right balance between them, and to harmonize them properly.

CHAPTER 3

High and low self-esteem

It is a case of learning these inner languages.
A great part of existence
happens between the self and the self.
So explore the territory
and get the most out of it.

— JEAN-LOUIS SERVAN-SCHREIBER

SELF-ESTEEM: A WAY OF LOOKING AT THE SELF, TALKING TO THE SELF AND FEELING THE SELF

Self-esteem reflects how we look at ourselves, at the words we use to speak of ourselves, and at the emotions and feelings we experience about ourselves.

Contemporary authors do not agree on the definition of self-esteem, which is often considered as a sort of psychological catch-all. Is there a way of formulating a definition of self-esteem that is at once concrete, beneficial and measurable? Self-esteem reflects how we look at ourselves, at the words we use to speak of ourselves, and at the emotions and feelings we experience about ourselves. These reveal what kind of esteem we have for our being and for our person, as well as for our abilities or performances.

Our responses to the following questions will indicate how much or how little self-esteem we have:

- How do I look at myself and my aptitudes — that is, what image do I have of these two aspects of my being?
- What do I say about my person and my aptitudes? How do I speak to myself?
- What are my emotions and feelings towards my person and my aptitudes?

We will thus discover the esteem in which we hold our person and our aptitudes thanks to visual (V), auditory (A),

We have the power to modify our perceptions of our person and of our aptitudes.

and emotional (K, for kinesthetic) perceptions. These reference points and norms allow us to evaluate the esteem we have for ourselves.

We become conscious of our interior landscape by examining the representations we have of ourselves: visual (for example, I see myself in a positive light); auditory – the content and tone of my inner dialogue (for example, I tell myself that I'm intelligent); and kinesthetic, or the range of emotions and feelings I experience as I think about myself (for example, I feel kindly towards myself). As we will see, self-esteem never refers to something magic, vague or abstract, but to many concrete perceptions.

Let's go one step further. In fact, we have the power to modify our perceptions of our person and of our aptitudes. For example, if we see ourselves only in the context of fault, we can change that. If we tend to speak harshly to ourselves, we can easily replace those words with encouraging ones. If we feel down, we can convert these depressing emotions into positive, enthusiastic ones by modifying our posture and breathing. It is possible to improve the mental perceptions we have of ourselves. We don't have to accept them as if we were powerless before them.

CRITERIA OF HIGH AND LOW SELF-ESTEEM

Your thoughts have made you what you are,
and they will make you what you will become, starting today.

— CATHERINE PONDER

How do we know if we have high or low self-esteem? The response can be found in the positive or negative way we see, speak to and feel about ourselves. First, let's look at self-esteem for the person, and then at self-esteem for competence.

SELF-ESTEEM FOR THE PERSON

What is my inner perspective on my person?

High self-esteem begins with a benevolent view of ourselves. To know the difference between a positive, kind view of ourselves, and a negative, unkind attitude, answer these questions: "Do I value or put down the physical image I have of myself? Do I like my physical appearance? Do I hate it?" Sometimes the disgust we feel towards ourselves is related to a single physical trait that we presume is ugly or deformed. Some people focus on this and lose sight of the big picture of their physical and moral appearance. They judge themselves and put themselves down because of a minor imperfection. This is typical of teenagers who see nothing but pimples on their faces.

Those who esteem themselves tend to see themselves as likable people in social relationships. Moreover, they believe that others consider them worthy of respect and love. In contrast, those who don't esteem themselves will never be able to believe that they deserve others' love and respect.

The degree of self-esteem we have depends on how much we value ourselves and our personal qualities. It does not come from comparing ourselves with others, but can be measured only against our own progress. Thus, someone who has high self-esteem will say to themselves, "I see myself as more tolerant, more enterprising, more likable than I was." On the other hand, those with low self-esteem tend to base their judgments about themselves on comparisons with others, which is almost always to their own disadvantage.

The degree of self-esteem we have depends on how much we value ourselves and our personal qualities.

*People who have
high self-esteem
speak to themselves
in understanding
tones.*

How do I talk about myself?

*You will learn to listen to your internal voice
and to follow only the path of joy.*

— RAMTHA

The questioning of the self covers the whole of our inner dialogue about our physical traits, qualities, values, and so on. People who have high self-esteem speak well about themselves. People with low self-esteem criticize themselves severely; sometimes they even wound themselves further.

The tone of voice we use to speak to ourselves has a profound influence on our self-esteem. A harsh, severe tone produces feelings of fear and distress, while a gentle, compassionate tone elicits tenderness and kindness towards the self. How we react to a mistake or a failure is very revealing. People with low self-esteem tend to heap on reproaches, in the tone of a critical parent. Their inner dialogue replays old tapes of humiliating and degrading phrases. They dramatize the situation, as though their whole personality was stained by some hidden and incurable vice. On the other hand, people who have high self-esteem speak to themselves in understanding tones, and say comforting things to themselves. They see in their errors or their failures an opportunity to discover what they shouldn't do to reach their goals.

People who esteem themselves are able to handle evaluations and criticisms. Because they know themselves well, they are able to give each of these commentaries the value they deserve. They understand that some are more relevant than others, and are suspicious of definitions that reduce them to only one thing: "You're nothing but ..." or "You're only good for ...." People who have poor self-esteem are vulnerable to the judgments of others and give them too much credibility.

Our convictions

The convictions we hold about ourselves have evolved in response to happy or unhappy experiences in our lives. They represent the effect of tenacious fixed thoughts that are inscribed in our affective memories. When we live through situations similar to those that originally gave rise to these thoughts, they rise to the surface and we repeat them to ourselves. These thoughts are of two types: depressing and invigorating. Some people, in the face of failure or a stinging rejection, have a tendency to blow the event up out of proportion, a reaction that becomes the general rule. They say to themselves in a pessimistic tone, " I know that they're out to get me"; "These things only happen to me"; "I was born unlucky." Those who have built up optimistic beliefs tell themselves instead, "Yes, I blew it, but this too will pass. I'm convinced that I was born under a lucky star, and that one day I'll succeed."

Some people express their beliefs through metaphors, which makes them even more persuasive. Compare, for example, these two metaphors: "My life is a journey full of pitfalls" and "My life is bursting with potential." It's not hard to see which metaphor promotes healthy self-esteem and which promotes low self-esteem and pessimism.

False identifications

Many people identify themselves with one of their positive qualities or faults (I'm generous), with some part of their body (I'm hard of hearing), with one of their faculties (I'm intelligent), with a societal role (I'm a mechanic), with a talent (I'm an artist), with an addiction (I'm an alcoholic), and so on. The

The convictions we hold about ourselves have evolved in response to happy or unhappy experiences in our lives.

One way of transforming our emotional state is to modify our posture.

unconscious and abusive use of the verb "to be" has restrictive and oppressive effects on how we value ourselves.

It is always preferable to use *have* or another verb to describe our attributes. Identifying ourselves with only one aspect of who we are tends to define us exclusively by this aspect and limits our ability to see ourselves differently. If we describe ourselves as being "generous" without saying anything more, this unbalanced identification keeps us from cultivating the opposite qualities, such as frugality and prudence in giving of ourselves. We could replace the affirmations listed above with "I've cultivated generosity"; "I have difficulty hearing"; "I have been given good intelligence"; "I practise the trade of mechanic"; "I exercise the profession of artist"; "I have an addiction to alcohol."

What emotions do I feel about myself?

It is possible to identify our emotions about ourselves, whether they are debilitating or inspiring. They are often the consequences of how we see ourselves, and of our dialogue with ourselves. What is important is to keep from being enslaved to a particular emotional state.

One way of transforming our emotional state is to modify our posture. We can change a depressed attitude, which is shown in a tired demeanour, a bent posture, and shallow breathing by assuming an energetic attitude, adopting upright posture and breathing deeply.

A second way of mastering our emotions and feelings is to express them. I start by identifying them, whatever they are: joy, sorrow, enthusiasm, anger, love, and so on. Then I ask myself what message they carry. Once I understand the message, I express the emotion and apply it to myself to eliminate the cause. For example, I am frustrated: I am conscious of my frustration when I listen to my body, because the body does not lie. Confident of the message of frustration, I choose whether to express it. People with strong self-esteem will choose to express it. This will give them a chance to eliminate the source of the frustration. People with low self-esteem will do the opposite; they will hold back their emotions and feelings so they no longer feel them; they will hide them in their bodies, or project them onto others; above all, they do not want to take responsibility for them.

A third way of dealing with our emotions is to ask ourselves, "Do I have a joyful, optimistic outlook on life or do I have a tendency to pessimism and defeatism?" Becoming conscious of our attitudes towards the difficulties of life gives us the means to manage our emotional states.

A final way of changing our emotional state is knowing how to make firm decisions so that a situation does not deteriorate. People who have low self-esteem have trouble making decisions: the spectre of making a wrong choice haunts them. They weigh the pros and cons without reaching any conclusions, and they imagine the worst consequences if they make a mistake.

People who have self-confidence see decision-making as a process that unfolds in time. They take the time to clarify their options, to understand what is at stake, and to discuss various aspects of the issues. Only after they have done this work do they take stock of their deep feelings about these options before choosing one. Throughout the process, they give themselves chances to revisit their decision.

People who have self-confidence see decision-making as a process that unfolds in time.

41

*People who are
confident in their
own aptitudes
generally have a
positive vision of
their future.*

SELF-ESTEEM FOR OUR APTITUDES AND COMPETENCE

How do I see my dreams becoming reality?

People who are confident in their own aptitudes generally have a positive vision of their future. When they dream about completing a project, they create a clear image of their success and are enthusiastic even before they begin. They anticipate the stages through which the project will be realized; they bear lightly the tension between what is and what is not yet. They persevere in their plan to the end, not becoming discouraged by the difficulties they encounter but remaining confident that they can overcome them. Failures or false starts are energizing, seen as challenges to be overcome.

In contrast, people with low self-esteem are paralyzed by the possibility of failure or error. Even the thought of a potential failure discourages them; they imagine beforehand all the obstacles that might plague their path and abandon projects before even beginning them. They are obsessed with past failures, which only reinforces their apprehensions. They go around in circles, and their predictions of failure or lack of success become self-fulfilling prophecies. The only consolation they can find is to tell themselves, "I knew it."

How do I speak with myself about my potential and my successes?

*Simply put, the words that you use
to describe your experience
become your experience.*

— ANTHONY ROBBINS

If we have high self-esteem, we can say to ourselves, "I have the ability to …; I am going to succeed; I know how to do this; I'm going to ask for advice; I acknowledge that I don't have to succeed the first time." Such an inner dialogue allows us to stay motivated and to bring our projects to completion.

Low self-esteem engages in an opposite kind of dialogue: "I'm not going to succeed; I'll never get to the end. I'm haunted by past mistakes. What's the use?" It is hardly surprising that such defeatist attitudes sap people's energies rather than motivating them. The best way to resist this latent pessimism is by learning to recognize even our smallest successes and to build up our confidence gradually.

Self-esteem reinforces a realistic sense of our limits. To overcome a sense of inferiority, some people succumb to delusions of grandeur: they dream of the impossible. Believing that they are capable of great exploits and brilliant creative work, they raise the bar too high and eventually are crippled by the impossibility of the task.

Self-esteem reinforces a realistic sense of our limits.

How do I feel about my aptitudes?

The key to a passionate life
is to trust in the energy within us and to follow it.

— SHAKTI GAWAIN

People who have healthy self-esteem are proud of their successes, however small these may be. Not only do they appreciate what they have achieved, but they also graciously accept other people's admiration. They keep their stockpile of congratulations full; they even take the initiative to celebrate themselves. They feel ready to face new challenges. They develop a taste for risk, confident that it is always possible to succeed. For them,

Studies on self-esteem show that people with low self-esteem take many fewer risks in order to protect their ego from errors or potential failure.

success leads to more success. These successes increase their confidence in the future and in their destiny as "winners."

At the opposite end of the spectrum, people with low self-esteem are never satisfied with their achievements. They are shackled by fear and indecision and severely criticize what they have accomplished. It's as though they keep hearing their parents or teachers saying, "You could have done better." They back off from positive recognition, or if they accept it, they minimize the import of what they've done: "I don't deserve any praise; the others did it all." "Anybody could have done it." "You people work well, too."

Studies on self-esteem show that people with low self-esteem take many fewer risks in order to protect their ego from errors or potential failure. Fearing that others will criticize them, they avoid public performances as much as possible.

Even success is seen as threatening. They dread setbacks and fear being unable to remain equal to the task. Following their successes, they imagine shouldering heavier responsibilities. They experience high levels of stress. Some people feel so stressed by the thought of success that they will do anything to sabotage their good fortune. We could say that they have "anxious happiness."

Here is a table that lays out the characteristics of high and low self-esteem in chart form.

HIGH AND LOW SELF-ESTEEM
FOR OUR PERSON

People with high self-esteem	People with low self-esteem
Like their bodies	Focus on faults
Appreciate their qualities	Accentuate faults
Tend not to compare themselves with others	Tend to compare themselves with others, to their own disadvantage
Show their originality	Are happy to imitate others
Presume they are loved by others	Are suspicious of how others see them, because they presume they will be hostile
Speak to themselves kindly	Are very critical of themselves and give themselves bad names
Listen to the criticisms of others, and decide whether they are pertinent	Are extremely sensitive to criticism from others, and are overly preoccupied with it
Console themselves when they make mistakes or experience failure	Blame themselves for their errors and failures
Use many metaphors of fulfillment to describe life	Hold negative opinions on life
Reject false identifications that people give them	Accept false identifications that are pinned on them
Walk tall and are self-assured	Look defeated and depressed
Accept their emotions and know how to express them	Reject their emotions and repress them
Know how to make good decisions using an effective methodology	Are never able to make the least decision; always hesitant

HIGH AND LOW SELF-ESTEEM FOR OUR APTITUDES

People who have self-confidence	People who lack self-confidence
Have a positive and optimistic view of their projects	Have a negative and defeatist view of their projects
Persevere despite obstacles and failures	Give up when faced by the least obstacle or failure
Keep up an optimistic and positive dialogue with themselves	Keep up a pessimistic and negative dialogue with themselves
Are confident they will succeed	Dread failure
Take risks	Take no risks
Remember past successes	Remember failures
Welcome the compliments and praise of others	Are suspicious of compliments and praise
Feel stimulated by new experiences	Feel comfortable in routine
Are confident that they can handle what is entrusted to them	Fear they won't be able to handle what is asked of them.
Ask for help and are confident they will receive it	Are uncomfortable asking for help
Look for challenge and adventure	Look for security, first and foremost
Like to respond to challenges such as speaking in public	Fear being in the public eye
Are encouraged by successes	Feel stressed by success

CHAPTER 4

Acquiring self-esteem

Some people believe that self-esteem is not learned. "Either you have it or you don't," they claim. Psychological research shows the contrary: self-esteem can be taught according to the rhythm and temperament of each child. Parents and teachers have the noble task of helping children acquire healthy self-esteem and become more independent at the same time. In the beginning, children depend closely on the reaction of significant adults in order to come to know and esteem themselves. These people act as mirrors for the children; little by little, they discover their self through the looks, actions, and behaviour of their parents. The children discover their ego, the centre of their consciousness and its interpretations, and ultimately acquire a proper sense of themselves.

Parents and teachers have the noble task of helping children acquire healthy self-esteem and become more independent at the same time.

If the reactions of their parents and teachers towards them are true and correct, children will learn to trust this reflection of themselves. But if their caregivers reflect a distorted image, children will form a false sense of self-esteem.

In adolescence, young people try to break away from the first circle of influence, that of parents and relatives, by trying to find reference points in their peer groups. Until they reach maturity, they work at conforming to this group's behaviour. They continue constructing an outer appearance that will allow them to be accepted and will affirm their sense of belonging. They create for themselves a persona or ideal self that will be socially accepted. Their sense of self-esteem is conditioned by others, who have become their point of comparison. When they reach maturity, they undertake the immense task of liberating themselves from their social masks to become more autonomous individuals.

Because the first influence on children is the attitudes and behaviours of their parents, teachers and other significant adults,

Educators' actions must allow children to feel accepted in their persons, their being, their emotions, their thoughts, and their judgments.

I will first set out here the pedagogical principles that promote self-esteem in children. These same principles are valuable at all stages of life.

IDEAL CONDITIONS FOR LEARNING SELF-ESTEEM

As you move forward, you dig out and create the riverbed into which the stream of your descendants will throw themselves and flow.

— NIKOS KAZANTZAKIS

I will avoid speaking here about mistreatment, manipulation by ridicule and shame, violence and negligence, and sexual abuse, and limit myself to the pedagogical factors that promote the acquisition and growth of self-esteem. To do this, I will summarize the principles used by Stanley Coopersmith in his book *The Antecedents of Self-Esteem*. He recommends five attitudes for educators of children:

a. Educators' actions must allow children to feel accepted in their persons, their being, their emotions, their thoughts, and their judgments. Even if they must show disapproval for faulty behaviours, they accept the child's emotions and ideas. At the same time, they indicate to the child that despite their misconduct, it is their person that counts most in their eyes.

b. Parents must give children definite, precise rules of conduct. They will establish realistic limits for the child's actions, for it is not good that children be left totally to themselves. Children will thus feel secure, thanks to this watchful framework. Furthermore, educators will learn to bend the rules as children demonstrate signs of maturity.

c. Educators will respect the person and the rights of the child. They will avoid ridiculing them, putting them down, withholding affection or using violence. They will respond to the children's needs and aspirations according to the values and limits that they will try to instill within their family life.

d. Educators will make clear to children their heightened but reasonable expectations, which are proportionate to the child's capacities. Above all they will encourage the children's efforts and demonstrate their confidence that children can improve their conduct and performance.

e. Educators will demonstrate healthy self-esteem. They will strive to model self-respect and self-confidence. This will encourage children to imitate their educators and to learn self-esteem from them. This daily example will in fact prove to be the best pedagogy for teaching children self-esteem.[4]

THE EFFECTIVENESS OF ATTENTION AND AFFECTION FOR ACQUIRING SELF-ESTEEM

To cultivate self-esteem, the school of transactional analysis places much importance on attention and affection. Affection and attention are not a kind of magic potion, but they do provide the three conditions conducive to stimulating self-esteem: the recipients, be they children or adults, must be able to see the meaning of the gesture, accept it and be nourished by it.

First, the person must perceive the meaning of the sign of affection and attention. The one who offers it must do so convincingly and unambiguously. A quick handshake that just brushes the fingertips and lacks warmth is neither convincing nor unambiguous.

Second, the person receiving these signs of affection and attention must be open to receiving them. Too many people feel

To cultivate self-esteem, the school of transactional analysis places much importance on attention and affection.

Freely given signs of attention, such as a kind word, a gesture of hospitality or a joyful attitude make us feel recognized, appreciated, valued — indeed, loved.

unable to accept compliments without becoming defensive. They are clearly ill at ease. They change the topic of conversation; they wait for the criticism to follow the compliment. Some people interpret every sign of affection or kind word as threatening.

Third, if a sign of affection or attention is to promote someone's self-esteem, the person must be able to be nourished by it — that is, allow themselves to be touched by it, add it to their store of positive experiences, and remember it during painful moments.

Let us look more concretely at some signs of attention and affection that can promote every person's esteem for their self and their aptitudes.

SIGNS OF ATTENTION AND AFFECTION THAT PROMOTE PERSONAL SELF-ESTEEM

The feeling of being one's self justifies our existence, that is the highest point of joy that love brings, however little it would be real.

— JEAN-PAUL SARTRE

Here are the freely given signs of attention and affection that support self-esteem for the person who learns to accept them and profit from them as though they were a bank account full of hugs and caresses.

Unconditional signs of attention

Freely given signs of attention, such as a kind word, a gesture of hospitality or a joyful attitude make us feel recognized, appreciated, valued — indeed, loved. Someone who, on entering or leaving, greets us, shakes our hand, smiles, taps us on the shoulder or welcomes us creates a joyful, comfortable dynamic.

We say to ourselves, "I have been made to feel at home; I am important and valuable in this person's eyes."

Louis Evely compares the effects of these attitudes and kindly gestures to a resurrection:

Has no one ever resurrected you?

Has no one ever spoken to you, pardoned you,

loved you enough to raise you up?

Have you never participated in resurrections?

Have you never raised up someone?

Have you experienced the power of life that springs forth

in a smile, an act of forgiveness, a welcome?

How we speak to and listen to people can dramatically affect their self-esteem.

Paying attention to and listening to others' emotions and feelings

How we speak to and listen to people can dramatically affect their self-esteem. A mother once asked a psychologist if she should start talking to her baby, who was two months old. The psychologist responded, "You're six months behind!" The simple fact of speaking to someone shows that we are interested in them. Listening to them and taking their feelings into account means that we accept and respect their emotional world. Not only do they feel listened to, they also feel understood and valued.

Even in a case where we discipline or reprimand someone, we must respect their feelings and avoid humiliating them. Parents must sometimes temper the enthusiasm of their children, but always in a ways that will allow the children to feel that their emotions are accepted.

Respecting what others feel helps create and maintain healthy self-esteem in them. Saying, "I see that you are angry with your sister, but I forbid you to hit her as you did," respects a child's emotions but sets clear guidelines for behaviour.

Puberty and mid-life are the most significant life transitions in terms of self-esteem.

Celebrating anniversaries and rites of passage

Marking birthdays and other significant rites of passage encourages self-esteem. Celebrating a birthday speaks to the person themselves, and is a sign of how much they are loved and valued. It is not a reward for good behaviour. I have met parents who punished a child by not giving him a birthday cake and presents. They had completely misunderstood the meaning of a birthday!

Puberty and mid-life are the most significant life transitions in terms of self-esteem. I have counselled many people who carry with them painful memories of not having been celebrated when they graduated, left home or received a promotion.

Signs of affection

Showing affection to a young person by touching them, particularly when the gesture is accompanied by positive words, promotes the development of self-love. Caring for a baby by bathing, changing diapers, feeding, and rocking not only contributes to their well-being, but reassures and values their very being. The neuroses that afflict some adults arise from the absence of these early signs of tenderness. The biggest mistake a parent can make is to use such privileged moments of caring for a child (mealtimes or bath times, for example) to scold or punish the child for misbehaving earlier in the day.

Signs of affection – kisses, hugs, and cuddles – bestowed generously cultivate self-love within a child.

They allow him or her to think, "Others show that they love me; therefore I must be loved and lovable." On the other hand, signs of affection given to a child or an adult only when they are obedient, clean or hard-working will make them think,

"Only when I'm good can I feel that I'm truly lovable and loved."

Unfortunately, some parents are uncomfortable showing their affection through touch. We see this particularly in fathers who, more or less consciously obsessed by the incest taboo, deny their sons and daughters normal displays of affection. Some mothers also repress their desire to show affection, particularly to their sons. By overzealously reporting charges of incest or inappropriate touching, the media has contributed to the creation of a climate of suspicion. Ultimately, it is children who pay the price: they find themselves without tender, warm, kindly contacts with adults.

We must remember that even healthy signs of affection and attention may be misinterpreted, however, and be sensitive to this reality.

HOW TO ACQUIRE AND MAINTAIN SELF-ESTEEM FOR OUR ABILITIES

Signs of attention for performance and creativity

Paying attention to their academic performance, work, initiative, and creativity nourishes a sense of competence in children and adults alike.

Attention from those in charge stimulates and encourages young people, improving their output and their behaviour. A simple remark made in passing, such as "I see that you've done your homework" or "You've done a good job," fosters a child's pride and encourages him or her to keep on far better than material rewards do. Unfortunately, far too many parents, teachers, and employers either don't believe in or don't trust the positive effect of words and signs of praise.

Paying attention to their academic performance, work, initiative, and creativity nourishes a sense of competence in children and adults alike.

It is important to give direction and guidance in a positive way.

Often, they limit themselves to rewarding work well done with money. I have seen parents go so far as to pay their children for doing chores and homework, which deprives them of taking pride in carrying out their responsibilities with dignity. Material rewards can't replace admiration and attention. When a child's performance is never recognized, motivation gradually decreases. Over time, children in this situation become discouraged, lack interest, neglect their work, and end up feeling like salaried strangers in their own home.

Discourage bad behaviour

Many parents and teachers fail to realize that their "don't" comments only reinforce a lack of discipline. I learned this from my own experience when I was teaching. I tended to pay a lot of attention to students who were disruptive. Without meaning to, I was encouraging their lack of discipline, giving them my attention by singling them out. Instead, I should have noted the tiniest amount of progress in their behaviour instead of making a big deal out of their inappropriate behaviour.

Likewise, it is important to give direction and guidance in a positive way. Presenting them in a negative way encourages the forbidden behaviour, because the imagination does not perceive the negation. Saying, "Please remain silent" rather than "Don't talk" offers a positive option.

If I tell you not to think about the colour red, you will immediately note that the colour red appears in your imagination, even before you can obey my words. You will therefore find it hard to get rid of this image. If I don't want my listeners to see red, I should say, "Think of green!"

How to give compliments

Knowing how to compliment and thank someone promotes the development of their esteem for their behaviour. Avoid exaggerated or evaluative comments, such as "You're a genius" or "You're an angel," as well as comments that set up comparisons, such as "You're better at _____ than your brother." Such messages create more stress than anything else. Formulate positive comments using "I" statements: "I'm proud of your work" or "I'm happy that you succeeded." These types of compliments avoid putting too much pressure on the recipient.

A sensitive way of giving compliments is to use words that reflect the child's joy: "You're happy you succeeded!" or "You're glad you won!" Reflecting these feelings celebrates the success.

A sensitive way of giving compliments is to use words that reflect the child's joy.

Expose the child to a variety of activities

The Québécois film *Les vrais perdants* [The Real Losers] tells the story of children who are enslaved to their parents' ambition. First we see a little girl of modest talent submissively practising piano for her mother's glory; then we meet a little boy who goes all out to learn the art of playing hockey to satisfy his father's pride in being a sportsman. Instead of choosing for your children, present a wide range of activities so they can choose one or two that appeal to them. Insist that a child stick to something for at least four or five months once they have made their choice, even if at first they don't get into it.

Develop initiative and creativity

In her book *Winning at Parenting,*[5] parenting expert Barbara Coloroso suggests the following approach when a child does something wrong: help him or her understand their mistake or what they did wrong; ask them to find and describe a solution to the problem; and discuss the feasibility of the solution with

Signs of affection are not earned or deserved. They are freely given.

them. This approach develops the child's initiative, hands-on knowledge, responsibility and, eventually, wisdom.

Be careful not to mix messages

Signs of affection and attention have different goals: encouraging self-esteem of the person, or self-esteem for abilities. Being present to the other, speaking tender words, listening to feelings, and giving kisses and cuddles all promote personal self-esteem. Recognizing the other's accomplishments, complimenting them, thanking them, congratulating them, and giving them gifts promote self-esteem for their abilities.

What happens if signs of affection are confused with signs of attention? There is a risk of misunderstanding. Let's take the example of a mother who hugs her children only when they do chores around the house. From this the children may conclude, "I am loved (or I feel lovable) only when I do something for others." They will feel loved, but for the wrong reasons. Signs of affection are not earned or deserved. They are freely given.

Another common example of how things can go wrong happens when one person in a couple uses intimacy to reward their partner's performance at work or at home. Such an approach interferes with the true purpose of the sexual relationship. It no longer expresses conjugal love, but simply compensation.

There is a great risk that the person to whom we show signs of admiration or attention instead of signs of affection will feel angry and frustrated that they aren't loved for themselves. In therapy, some people complain of a lack of affection. For example, they express their bitterness at never having been hugged by their parents, but only praised for their hard work at school, their perfect behaviour, and the amount of work they do. One person confided to me that when he was a child his mother saw him as a "performing dog." Many men and women, because they have never been loved for who they are, have ruined their careers or relationships through bulimia, sexual abuse, drugs or excessive drinking. All of these activities, which suggest great immaturity, are clumsy attempts to satisfy a frustrated need to be loved.

Of themselves, signs of affection increase self-love, while signs of attention develop confidence in our abilities. A balance between the two is essential to enable people to reach maturity.

Of themselves, signs of affection increase self-love, while signs of attention develop confidence in our abilities.

CHAPTER 5

Affirming the self

*Anything that is not expressed
is imprinted on the self.*

— Origen

WHAT IS THE AFFIRMATION OF THE SELF?

People often confuse self-esteem, which springs from our inner life, with affirmation of the self, which is an expression of our inner life. Understanding affirmation of the self is important because it requires special social skills. Self-affirmation consists of externalizing our inner world of images, intimate dialogues, feelings, thoughts, needs, values, and spiritual aspirations. In the language of neurolinguistic programming, we can say that self-esteem constitutes an inner mini-program, whereas self-affirmation corresponds to an external macro-program using verbal and non-verbal behaviours: words, tone of voice, appearance, posture, attitudes, gesture, dress, and so on. And yet we cannot isolate affirmation from communication in general, of which affirmation is an element.

Self-affirmation is part of a constant exchange with one or more listeners who react to a message.

The communication cycle

Self-affirmation is part of a constant exchange with one or more listeners who react to a message. The process is continuous. The reactions of the receiver provoke a new reaction and a new self-affirmation on the side of the sender. This is the sense of Camus's statement that "To know ourselves better, we must affirm ourselves more." Self-affirmation allows us to know ourselves better: first, because of the reactions of another, and then, because of our own reactions.

Like self-esteem, self-affirmation is an art that is learned and developed.

Sender	Receiver
The sender sends a message. ☞ (Self-affirmation)	The receiver perceives it in his/her own way. (Selective hearing) ⇩
⇧ The communication begins all over again.	The receiver interprets the message according to his/her own self-esteem. ⇩
⇧ The sender receives the message from the receiver and interprets it according to his/her own self-esteem.	He/She reacts verbally or non-verbally. (self-affirmation) ☜

What makes self-affirmation difficult

Self-affirmation can be difficult for many reasons, including lack of family models, childhood orders to keep quiet, a sense of impotence, severe shyness, an unreceptive or even hostile milieu, the inability to speak out or express emotions, fear of being judged, or an exaggerated sense of discretion. However, all these handicaps to expression can be corrected through adequate learning and practice.

Like self-esteem, self-affirmation is an art that is learned and developed.

What self-affirmation is not

Self-affirmation should not be equated with emotional catharsis, with an incoherent and unreflected expression of our person. In fact, appropriate self-affirmation asks us to be as coherent and honest as possible with our life experience in our social context. For example, we vary our approach depending on the audience: we do not use the same tone or assume the same attitude when speaking to a child as we do when discussing a sensitive issue with an adversary.

FORMS OF SELF-AFFIRMATION

Caring for our physical appearance

A self-assured person does not hang their head, avoid looking another in the eye, slouch, breathe shallowly or seem unsteady on their feet. Such a physical appearance betrays a serious lack of assurance. People who affirm themselves instead stand tall, have a relaxed expression and breathe calmly, speak with a firm voice and have their feet firmly planted on the ground. It has been said that the internal influences the external, but the opposite is equally true: good posture, an expressive look, a firm voice, and a relaxed attitude can help us feel more confident.

Fashion exerts enormous social pressure, especially on those who see themselves as unattractive. Some young people who cannot afford designer labels or the latest styles may feel excluded from the group; they may even feel their lives are ruined. Fashion cannot be ignored, but neither should it enslave us. It can never replace such qualities such as spontaneity, simplicity, openness and honesty.

Affirming our right to exist

Affirming ourselves means first showing that we have the right to exist. Only we can defend our inviolable rights — what Maurice Zundel calls the "inviolability of conscience."

Affirming ourselves means taking our place in society. Some people try to disappear into the background. Such was the case of a colleague of mine who stayed silent during our group meetings. When I asked why he did not speak, he answered

People who affirm themselves stand tall, have a relaxed expression and breathe calmly.

Only we know our daily needs and our deepest aspirations.

that he did not feel important among us, and thought that his ideas were not worth expressing. He preferred to remain quiet and unnoticed. I wanted to find out more about his silence. He confided to me that when he was very young his parents had forbidden him to speak in front of adults. This prohibition had followed him into his adult life. In response to my invitation, he decided that from then on, he would participate in the meetings. He taught himself to ask questions and make brief remarks. As he gained self-assurance, he dared to share his ideas with the group.

Asking for what we need

Only we know our daily needs and our deepest aspirations. But many people do not dare to express themselves because they are afraid of rejection. Instead, they do not ask for anything.

One of the characteristic traits of self-affirmation is the ability to ask. One day I was astonished by the attitude of a friend from New York. He made constant demands of perfect strangers – asking passersby for the time, begging kids who were playing ball to pass to him, and even asking a child if he could have a lick of his ice cream cone! I was both fascinated and amazed by his audacity. He told me that people felt honoured to give him what he wanted. Then I was better able to understand this passage of the gospel: "Ask and it will be given to you; seek, and you will find; knock and it will be opened to you" (Matthew 7.7-8).

When people meet strong resistance to their requests, they may stop giving themselves permission to make them, or they may feel very awkward about it. They dread being refused and are haunted by various fears: fear of rejection, of ridicule, of powerlessness, of humiliation, of appearing to be dependent, of having to do the same in return. Even for people who dare to ask for things, these same fears may drive them to use ineffective strategies for making demands. For example, some people choose to make their partners guess their needs rather than present them directly, as if honest demands would destroy a romantic mood. This tactic is ineffective, however, as one partner cannot read the other's mind.

We develop the art of asking with practice.

Others allude to what they want, since they do not dare show their desire directly for fear that they be refused and will lose face. The woman who really wants to go to the movies but only points out to her husband that a particular film is playing will not always obtain the desired results. He may notice that the film interests her, but not realize she wants to see it at that time. Still others have the habit of complaining in order to make those close to them feel guilty, instead of clearly stating their needs. Finally, there are those who sabotage their request from the very beginning: they dare to ask, but quickly provide their listeners with reasons to refuse them: "Perhaps I'm asking too much: feel free to say no." These same people are often astonished when a refusal follows.

We develop the art of asking with practice. The following conditions assure its success:
- Be clear about what you're asking.
- Be convinced that what you're asking is valid.
- Ask with passion to get what you want.
- Before making your request, consider the habits and the personality of the one who will respond. (For example, don't ask until they have had their morning coffee!)
- Keep trying.

People also ask for signs of affection and attention. A student might ask a teacher who had highlighted only the mistakes

People with high self-esteem possess a whole repertoire of feelings and emotions that they learn to express appropriately.

in her paper whether he could congratulate her for the parts of her work that were done well. While it is appropriate to ask for signs of affection and attention, we cannot insist on them. The other always has the right to refuse. That is the golden rule in the life of a couple. When one partner asks for something, they must always give the other every freedom to respond in their own way and in their own time.

Practising expressing our feelings and emotions

One day I invited a friend who is also a psychologist to go canoeing. To my surprise, he curtly refused. The next day he told me that he was afraid of the water, but that he wanted to conquer his fear. I admired his humility and his openness. He confided later that he was working at expressing his emotions, even if he risked being judged as overly sensitive.

In general, men find it harder than women do to express certain feelings and emotions, such as tenderness, gentleness, fear, vulnerability, and exuberance. It's not that men don't feel these intensely, but many think expressing them is too feminine. They prefer to withdraw in silence into their caves, like lords wounded by life. Men often feel more at ease showing their strength, combativeness, anger, and pride, emotions that many women tend to repress.

People with high self-esteem possess a whole repertoire of feelings and emotions that they learn to express appropriately. Once expressed, these emotions create within us a free space that other emotions and feelings can occupy. Repressing feelings can result in inauthentic behaviour, damage health, and interfere with intimacy.

How to negotiate

Negotiation is the key to affirmation. When one person clearly formulates a request and the other responds by clearly proposing another request, the two parties must negotiate. Negotiation begins the moment two people take the time to express their needs and talk about them. Conflict of needs can be resolved as long as the two parties sincerely seek a way to resolve them. The art of negotiating requires those involved to agree that the outcome will please both parties. Negotiation is impossible when one party insists on proving himself or herself right and the other wrong.

The art of negotiating requires those involved to agree that the outcome will please both parties.

Learning to accept signs of attention and affection

Have you ever met someone who refuses to accept thanks, compliments or gestures of affection, or who tries to downplay them? Someone who seems allergic to any signs of attention or affection? These people often have poor self-esteem. Believing that they are unworthy of praise, they doubt the speaker's sincerity. In the past, I have had the habit of not savouring sufficiently the congratulations, thanks or signs of affection shown me. Was it embarrassment, modesty or misplaced independence? All are signs of poor self-esteem! Today I strive to welcome and enjoy signs of attention and affection. They enrich my "bank account of caresses" and strengthen my self-esteem.

Giving ourselves permission to refuse signs of attention and affection

Certain signs of attention and affection make us uncomfortable. When we believe that the giver is insincere, wanting to please at any price, or wants something in return, we have the right to refuse the signs of attention or affection that are

*Every time we say
"yes" to someone
when we want to
say "no," we break
faith with ourselves.*

offered, or to let the other person know that we are not taken in by them.

Giving ourselves permission to say "no" when it is appropriate to do so is a way of protecting our own freedom. As young people grow up, they sense the need to take their place in the world and preserve their autonomy. Parents are not always aware that they have less and less hold over their children. Even younger children do not always have to meet parental expectations. With great admiration I listened to a child say to his mother, who was insisting that he eat his soup: "The soup is good, and I know that you made it lovingly for me, but I'm full."

At a certain point, parents must cut the umbilical cord, especially with young adults who return home after an unsuccessful attempt at freedom. If the situation is urgent, parents do well to bail out their adult child, on condition that both parties negotiate the length of the stay. Maintaining a more detached relationship requires courage, and neither party needs to feel guilty for altering the dynamic in this way.

Every time we say "yes" to someone when we want to say "no," we break faith with ourselves. We can turn down a request graciously and preserve our relationship with the requester by following these steps:

- listen to the request,
- reformulate it to be sure you have understood it properly,
- explain why you cannot accept, and
- if possible, offer an alternative gesture in its place.

Expressing yourself in public

Many students don't let themselves ask questions in class. Even when they need clarification, they prefer to keep quiet.

Because of their feelings of inferiority, they may be afraid of looking stupid, appearing ridiculous, or disturbing the class or the teacher.

Statistics that describe our most common fears show that some people would "rather die" than speak in public. People who are new to their field, for example, may feel physically ill at the thought of all these people looking at them and listening to them. As a result, they lose their composure, imagining that their listeners will criticize them severely. In short, they make themselves afraid.

Conquering the fear of public speaking requires a forceful affirmation of the self.

Conquering the fear of public speaking requires a forceful affirmation of the self. This can be done! There are ways of overcoming stage fright:

- Take time to centre yourself and become calm, then visualize other situations where you did well.
- Practise speaking in a non-threatening environment: alone in front of a mirror, or by asking a question or giving your opinion in a small-group setting.
- Be familiar with the space where you will speak (make sure the microphone is working, ask for a lectern, etc.) and focus on your message beforehand.
- Give your talk, first outlining to the audience what you will say and then speaking slowly and clearly.

Once you summon the courage to take the plunge, you will feel proud of yourself.

CHAPTER 6

Self-esteem and our relationships with others

Whom do you love more?

Queen Malika and King Kosala were contemporaries of the Buddha. The queen had recently converted to Buddhism. The king had not, but he respected the religious convictions of his wife. Now, in the course of a very romantic evening, the king bent over the queen, looked at her tenderly and asked her, "Whom do you love most in all the world?" He was expecting that the queen would say, "You!" Instead, the queen replied, "Well, I love myself most in all the world." Surprised at this response, the king thought for a moment, and said to her, "I must tell you that I too love myself most in all the world." Since both of them were somewhat dismayed by the turn the conversation had taken, they went to seek the Buddha's enlightenment.

The Buddha congratulated them on asking such an important question. He told them that in fact each person loved himself or herself most in all the world. Then he added, "If you understand this truth, you will stop manipulating and exploiting each other. If you love yourselves, there will be no more competition between you. You will not need to defend your own worth, and by that very fact, you will not need to argue. If you love yourselves, you will free yourselves from the stumbling block of insisting that others love you.

"Speaking for myself, I need the love of others, but I can't order them to love me. If my need for love is not fulfilled by others, I reassure myself that I can love myself. Thus I leave others free to love me or not."

The Buddha continued his teaching: "To reach this ideal of self-esteem, you must abandon the notion that you are superior or inferior to others, or even their equal. If you're neither superior, inferior nor equal, what is left to you? The ideal is to remain yourselves. If you are yourselves without comparing yourselves to others, you enter into perfect communion with them."

— BUDDHIST LEGEND

Real self-love demands that we love others.

The link between love of self and love of others is well established. We cannot love others if we do not love ourselves. Often these two realities are set in opposition to each other, as if they were incompatible. Some people say that loving ourselves keeps us from loving others. People who do not understand authentic self-esteem claim that it's nothing but individualism, navel-gazing and selfishness. This is a common mistake in certain educational contexts or in spiritual formation. The truth is that the more we truly esteem ourselves, the more we will esteem others; the more we lack self-esteem, the more we will undervalue others.

THE GOLDEN RULE

The Buddhist legend recounted above echoes the golden rule of the Bible: "Love your neighbour as yourself." This positive statement also has a negative formulation: "Do not do to others what you do not want them to do to you." It is a paradox that love of others finds its source in love of self, and is in fact the measure of self-love. Real self-love *demands* that we love others.

The commentary of the great theologian Thomas Aquinas on the golden rule clearly affirms that priority of love of self over love of the other. Commenting on the passage of the gospel "Love your neighbour as yourself" (Matthew 22.39), Saint Thomas writes: "The love of self, as the model for love of others, is in principle more important than love of others."[6] All real love for others originates in self-love. Jesus' command continues to be relevant today.

DISASTROUS SOCIAL CONSEQUENCES OF LACK OF SELF-ESTEEM

Lack of self-esteem leads to antisocial behaviours such as lack of trust, defensiveness, isolation, over-dependence and manipulation. Forgiveness, the perfect gift of wounded love, becomes impossible if we do not love ourselves, if we fail to care for our own wounds.

Lack of confidence in others

The American comedian Groucho Marx used to joke: "I don't care to belong to any club that will have me as a member." People who do not make love of self a priority see themselves as unworthy of love. They doubt the sincerity of those who offer them signs of affection and attention. If they hate themselves, they expect to be humiliated and rejected.

A man whose wife systematically refused his compliments and caresses told their marriage counsellor, "She says she needs love and consideration, but when I give them to her, she rejects them." Paradoxically, this woman wrongly accused her husband of flirting with other women and said she didn't feel appreciated by him. Moreover, she became very jealous when he showed others signs of affection and attention. Her lack of self-esteem kept her from receiving her spouse's affection and admiration and being nourished by it.

Many people with low self-esteem live in constant contradiction with themselves. They want attention and tenderness, but do not feel ready to receive them because they cannot love themselves. It's as though they're standing right beside a stream dying of thirst.

Some will even choose a partner who will eventually abandon or reject them. If they find love, they will do everything in

People who do not make love of self a priority see themselves as unworthy of love.

71

People with poor self-esteem also become rigidly independent, fearing every form of dependence on others.

their power to sabotage it. They want constant reassurance; they cling to their lover; sometimes they are submissive, sometimes domineering. They reject their partner before their partner has even dreamt of rejecting them.

The tendency towards isolation and defensiveness

When people dislike themselves and have a heightened sense of their weaknesses, they live with an exaggerated fear that these weaknesses will be discovered. They become defensive, so no one will recognize their limits or see the least fault. They try to hide their mistakes and their fragility. They become very touchy, then aggressive, and prefer to isolate themselves rather than risk revealing their true colours.

People with poor self-esteem also become rigidly independent, fearing every form of dependence on others. To preserve this independence, they avoid the least contact with others, shutting themselves up in their ivory tower or escaping their isolation by creating artificial paradises such as overeating, drinking too much, or using drugs.

Excessive dependence

A lack of self-esteem can also produce the inverse of independence – that is, a strong, chronic affective dependence. People who follow this path need to stick to someone like glue, fall in love frequently, and impose intimacy on the other. They are incapable of solitude, but they have no authentic relationships or real friendships. They merge into everyone they meet to avoid being alone.

s w

Manipulating others by weakness or by domination

*The energy of the self remains imprisoned
as long as people believe that others
are responsible for their problems and finding the solutions.*

— SHAKTI GAWAIN

Eric Berne's well-known book *Games People Play* describes well how those who have neither self-esteem nor self-confidence manipulate others. There are two types: passive and active manipulators. The first look like weak people, victims; the second, like strong, powerful people who can "save" the world. The relational dynamic that results is called the Karpman triangle, after its creator:

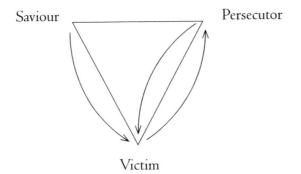

Saviour   Persecutor

Victim

This common social dynamic can be a destructive one for the people involved. The saviour becomes the victim of the person he or she was trying to help. Paradoxically, the saviour ends up persecuting the victim he or she was trying to save.

Passive manipulators look like perpetual victims who have no confidence in their talents or abilities. They get themselves into impossible situations from which they cry for help, attract-

Passive manipulators look like perpetual victims who have no confidence in their talents or abilities.

Active manipulators do not want to admit either their weaknesses or their limits.

ing the attention of the saviours, who feel sorry for them. They are bottomless wells. They ask for help especially when they are the only ones who can help themselves. They make impossible demands, such as "Help me to like myself" or "Make me happy."

Active manipulators do not want to admit either their weaknesses or their limits. They put forward a false image of strength and confidence. To boost themselves, they compulsively try to save "victims." They are dependent on the dependence of others, and eventually burn out. Once they run out of energy and strength, they get angry at the passive manipulators, overwhelm them with complaints, and even persecute them.

THE BENEFICIAL EFFECTS OF SELF-ESTEEM ON SOCIETY

Self-esteem is the basis for authentic social relationships

People who have high self-esteem don't need to conceal their thoughts, feelings, intentions, and values. They express them as authentically and honestly as possible. They try to be transparent, even in the most ordinary daily events. They avoid half-truths, white lies, keeping secrets, pretence, and showing off.

During a workshop I gave on self-esteem, participants did an exercise on integrity. They were asked to respond to this question: "If I had 10 per cent more honesty in my life, what would I say or do?" Here is a sampling of the responses:

- I would say openly to someone that they aggravate me and bother me.
- I would tell my husband the truth about my small purchases.

- I wouldn't laugh at jokes that I find stupid or racist.
- I would tell the whole truth about the products I sell.
- I would say "No" when I want to say "No."
- I'd say I'm sorry instead of trying to justify my mistakes.
- I wouldn't hide my frustration as I do so often.
- I wouldn't be afraid to apologize and make amends to someone I've hurt.
- I wouldn't hide my pain.
- I'd admit my weaknesses more easily.
- I wouldn't pretend to have news to share when I don't.
- Jealousy wouldn't keep me from giving compliments.

People who want to increase their self-esteem conquer their fear of showing who they really are.

People who want to increase their self-esteem conquer their fear of showing who they really are, becoming more honest and more transparent with those around them.

Self-esteem lets us enjoy solitude

To be attentive to others even as we keep our distance,
maintain a space,
for the less we are caught up by the other,
the more we can listen to them.

— MICHÈLE SALAMAGNE

Those who have a strong sense of self-esteem recognize the difference between isolation and solitude. Isolation is being closed to others out of fear of being invaded; solitude is a strategic retreat from social life to become more present to ourselves. Isolation happens when we develop a system of protection based on fear of others; solitude lets us experience inner peace. Isolation fears our vulnerability; solitude accepts vulnerability and intimacy with ourselves.

*The most
significant social
gestures are
forgiveness and
reconciliation.*

As strange as it may seem, solitude produces a deeper sense of presence to others. People who have experienced this sense of wholeness and peace are more able to be loving towards others.

Self-esteem allows us to enjoy an autonomy in our relationships that is life-giving

Self-esteem promotes autonomy by harmonizing the parts of the self with each other. When we are at peace with ourselves, we can assert ourselves serenely. In contrast, people who put themselves down are plagued by discordant interior voices.

Some people think, mistakenly, that being autonomous will keep them from being dependent on anyone or anything. But autonomy is not the opposite of dependence; the two can co-exist. In fact, those who enjoy a healthy autonomy choose to be with people with whom they can establish healthy relationships of dependence.

Self-respect and self-esteem make forgiveness possible

*If you cannot be compassionate towards yourself,
you will never be able to be compassionate towards others.*

– THICH NHAT HANH

The most significant social gestures are forgiveness and reconciliation. Without self-respect and self-esteem, real forgiveness would be impossible. The process of forgiveness requires that offended parties begin by becoming conscious of being wounded and take time to attend to their hurt feelings. They must experience true compassion for themselves before they can feel it for the person who hurt them. This is the pre-condition for all forgiveness.[7]

CONCLUSION

Healthy self-love and self-confidence are at the heart of human relationships. Without them, people tend to distrust and manipulate others. In contrast, people with high self-esteem do not overrate either their strengths or their weaknesses. They do not compare themselves with others. They express affection and give attention generously, and when they receive them from others, they do so with gratitude. They also know how to refuse such gestures when they seem insincere or phony. They avoid playing manipulative games that lock them into unhealthy dealings with others.

Healthy self-love and self-confidence are at the heart of human relationships.

CHAPTER 7

Illnesses associated with low self-esteem

Every kingdom divided against itself is laid waste.

— MATTHEW 12.5

All work on self-esteem aims to assure the conscious self of a greater autonomy – that is, the freedom to act based on one's own choices. To be autonomous is to be able to disengage from instinctual, social, and cultural conditioning that is projected onto the self. It also involves living our lives following the truest and deepest inclinations of our being, instead of blindly following the dictates of our persona, our social self. As autonomous beings, we make choices that reflect our identity and fulfill our personal mission.

I am convinced that it is possible to transform poor self-esteem into healthy self-esteem.

This chapter aims to sensitize the reader to the obstacles to self-esteem and autonomy. The descriptions of these illnesses serve as red flags, alerting us to both the illusions of the false self and deviations from self-esteem.

I am convinced that it is possible to transform poor self-esteem into healthy self-esteem. I will describe only the neuroses that affect the "I" or the self; I will not deal with psychoses.

THE FALSE SELF

On the edge of the conscious self lives the *persona* or social self whose function is to enable individuals to adapt to the expectations and real or imaginary demands of their milieu. Children quickly learn to respond to the expectations of their parents and other significant adults, to try to please them in order to be accepted. The normal development of the *persona* empowers them to live harmoniously with those around them, and spares them as many conflicts as possible. Children have a fundamental need to be recognized and to forge ties to their immediate community. They create these ties by obeying the

Some people become conscious of their false self when they are with people who are truly themselves.

rules and laws of the group, even if this means compromising some of their own tendencies or preferences.

But accidents do happen during the normal formation of the persona when their caregivers send mixed messages to the child or fail to respond to his or her basic needs. In such cases, children have difficulty adjusting. To survive, their only choice is to hide who they are and use defensive, rigid adaptation strategies.

To protect themselves, they will therefore adopt an accommodating exterior, a "false self," as Winnicott, a leading expert in child development, calls it.[8] The false self is born of these first failed efforts at adaptation caused by the frustrating and contradictory behaviour of the mother. Disturbed in this primary relationship by many disappointments, the child builds a protective wall. Instead of presenting a healthy persona, an adapted social self, the child tries to outsmart this world, which is experienced as intrusive, incoherent, and threatening. Far from being good for the conscious self, this unhealthy adaptation leads to the alienation of the true self.

Children – and, later, adolescents – construct from this point an armour-clad persona and no longer dare to express true feelings and emotions. They do all they can to reveal only what they think will be acceptable to and welcomed by those around them. Transactional analysis calls this survival tactic "racket feelings." Young people who follow this approach will use the manipulative manouevres that Eric Berne describes in *Games People Play.* The tragedy is that they miss an opportunity to develop authentic self-esteem.

Some people become conscious of their false self when they are with people who are truly themselves. Initially they have a vague feeling of being an imposter, and eventually realize that their manipulations are useless and even harmful.

Let us now examine the different neurotic disguises that false adaptations of the persona assume.

The narcissistic personality is a good example of a false self.

THE NARCISSIST

The narcissistic personality is a good example of a false self. Instead of having an accurate perception of what they are, narcissists are constantly preoccupied with their social image. They behave like Narcissus, the mythological character who fell so in love with his own face reflected in the water that he drowned trying to get a closer look at it. Legend has it that at the place where he fell, a flower called narcissus sprang up.

This is the case, for example, with a young man who feels that he exists only when he enjoys the attention of a woman. Watching the effect he has on his admirer gives him an intense feeling of satisfaction.

The narcissists' tragedy is that they believe they only really exist through the gaze of another. In other words, they are preoccupied with their image, especially the image the other sends back to them. At the same time, they are unable to really connect with another person and build an intimate relationship with them. They condemn themselves to living alone in a fantasy world.

The narcissistic personality's inability to have a real encounter is well illustrated by Oscar Wilde's ending to the myth of Narcissus. The mountain nymphs or goddesses, the oreads, arrive at the shore, only to find the lake transformed into a jar of tears.

"Why do you weep?" the goddesses asked.

"I weep for Narcissus," the lake replied.

Perfectionists are a good example of a lack of self-esteem.

"Ah, it is no surprise that you weep for Narcissus," they said, "for though we always pursued him in the forest, you alone could contemplate his beauty close at hand."

"But...was Narcissus beautiful?" the lake asked.

"Who better than you to know that?" the goddesses said in wonder. "After all, it was by your banks that he knelt each day to contemplate himself!"

The lake was silent for some time. Finally it said:

"I weep for Narcissus, but I never noticed that Narcissus was beautiful. I weep because, each time he knelt beside my banks, I could see, in the depths of his eyes, my own beauty reflected."[9]

THE PERFECTIONIST

Despite appearances to the contrary, perfectionists are a good example of a lack of self-esteem. Because they are unable to stay in touch with themselves, they are always worried about conforming to social norms and codes. That is where they find the ideal of perfection. They conceal from themselves even their smallest weakness or transgression, for they would be ashamed to be out of tune with their image of perfection. Always on high alert, they try to avoid the tiniest error in their work, or the most minor lapse in behaviour. In setting such high standards for themselves, they are in a constant state of stress. It is therefore hardly surprising that they are rigid and irritable towards themselves and those around them.

Perfectionists choose certain social virtues that they then try to perfect: cleanliness, discipline, steadiness, obedience, politeness, faithfulness, and so on. At the same time, they ignore other, equally important ones, such as cordiality, relaxation, generosity, tolerance, and flexibility. Carl Jung put it well when he said that he would rather be well-rounded than perfect. I remember a superior I had who was so carried away with discipline that he forgot the simple rules of civility and kindness. He would have been better off being less "perfect" and more "well-rounded." People who have high self-esteem accept everything in themselves, their gifts as well as their weaknesses. They don't aim for impeccable behaviour on every point.

In the long run, perfectionists cannot maintain the effort they put into fighting the emergence of their shadow (the deviant aspect of their personality). The psychic tension that results from continuously repressing their shadow will give rise to all kinds of painful reactions: obsessions, uncontrollable fears, prejudices, compulsive moral failures, to say nothing of psychological exhaustion and depression.[10]

THE PERSON OBSESSED WITH SELF-ESTEEM

A subtle form of narcissism seems to be very popular: exaggerated concern with the self.

A subtle form of narcissism seems to be very popular: exaggerated concern with the self. People in the clutches of this obsession cause themselves unnecessary trouble. They anguish over their health, dreaming only of rest and vacations. They worry that they are not making enough progress in acquiring self-esteem and are constantly concerned with their own personal fulfillment. They become hypersensitive, and even tend toward hypochondria.

This obsession with the self can cancel out any real self-fulfillment. Constant re-examination and turning back on the self are unhealthy approaches that often bring in their wake a kind of navel-gazing, in addition to damaging healthy physiological reflexes such as digestion and the rhythm of their heart. The development of the self becomes a burden. Instead of

Self-esteem has nothing to do with pride or a superiority complex.

thinking about living well, these people get wrapped up in a harmful examination of themselves and their actions. Often, because they were denied their basic needs early in life, they do not have enough confidence in the spontaneity of life, in their instincts and intuitions, in their desire to love and be loved.

THOSE WHO ARE PROUD

Some people associate self-esteem with pride. This is a serious error, based on a false understanding of self-esteem. Traditional morality defined the sin of pride in terms of an excessive sense of superiority that can lead to contempt for others. Psychologists more often speak in terms of a superiority complex. They would also argue that the disproportionate focus on the self comes from a deep sense of inferiority. In fighting a strong feeling of ineptitude, people who act proud seem arrogant and rude. Healing will come when they become conscious of and then accept their weaknesses and fragilities. Self-esteem has nothing to do with pride or a superiority complex. Only those who have poor self-esteem believe this to be the case.

THE PERSON WITH ARTIFICIAL SELF-ESTEEM

Another form of false self-esteem is found in people who think that they are very important because of their possessions or their influence. Having an expensive car or house, belonging to an exclusive club or living in an upscale neighbourhood, being a "personality," enjoying certain privileges, or having many sexual conquests inflates the ego to the point where they believe that they have healthy self-esteem. This is a dangerous illusion, because although there is nothing wrong with being proud of one's possessions and accomplishments, all these outer signs of success have nothing to do with self-esteem, which comes from internal sources.

We have only to note how few people who are rich, famous, and admired by the public really love and trust themselves. Many of them are so unhappy that they end up isolating themselves and trying to fill their existential emptiness with alcohol, drugs, shopping, and even thoughts of suicide.

Self-esteem, as we have seen, is the feeling of loving oneself, of being loved, of being competent and useful to others. It is above all the result of inner work.

Self-esteem is above all the result of inner work.

THE SEDUCER

Seducers use their charms to manipulate and dominate their conquests. Their devices disclose a serious lack of regard for themselves and their talents, and their ability to succeed in life. They prefer seduction to working hard at their job and earning others' approval for their efforts. Although they know they have the power to seduce, they lack the self-confidence to succeed in life. When they were very young, someone told them that good looks and charm were all they would need to be happy. They were never encouraged or guided to develop their aptitudes.

I knew a lovely, caring woman whose mother had always told her: "Beautiful women like us don't need to work. There will always be a prince charming to support us and support us well." Life showed her otherwise: her disappointments in love taught her that to have a good life, she had to depend on her own abilities, talents, and initiative.

*The helpless
cultivate a feeling
that is diametrically
opposed to self-
confidence.*

THE WORKAHOLIC

The workaholic's problem is the opposite of the seducer's. The early teachers of workaholics placed a lot of trust in them, giving them many challenges to meet, but neglecting to show them unstinting affection. These adults only hugged and praised them to reward good behaviour and success. Such children naturally confused signs of affection with success, and concluded that the love shown by people close to them is never freely given, but must to be earned through hard work. "If I work without taking a break, and if I accomplish what's expected of me to the point of forgetting my own needs and desires, others will love me," a workaholic would reason. These children confuse admiration and love, and their thirst for affection makes them work to excess. When they become adults, they will push themselves to burnout to try to meet the real or imagined expectations of others. The chronic frustration of their childhood need for tenderness leads them to convince themselves that they can never do enough.

THE HELPLESS PERSON

The helpless cultivate a feeling that is diametrically opposed to self-confidence. Their reasoning rests on the illusion that if they look like they're weak, stupid or incompetent, they will always find a good Samaritan who will come to their rescue. Expressions like "I can't do it" or "It's always my fault" can be heard on their lips. They are so convinced of their inability to succeed in almost every area that they see themselves as victims of fate. Before they begin a project, they figure they are already defeated; they are haunted by failure and always find good excuses — outside themselves — to explain their lack of success. They hold to the same old defeatist story: "What's the use?" In short, they apply all their intelligence to avoiding tasks instead of trying hard to accomplish them.

Many helpless people believe that their problem is inherited. One woman who had had several unhappy love affairs confided, "I'm convinced that I have a congenital defect; fate is making me chase after men who will hurt me." She truly believed that she had been born into a tragic destiny. People like this are certain that they are responsible for all their unhappiness, that they are condemned to fail, and that things will always turn out badly for them. Therapists working in the area of self-esteem can help them overcome these misguided beliefs.

Many helpless people believe that their problem is inherited.

THE PERSON WHO IS ASHAMED

First, we must distinguish between guilt and shame. People feel guilt when they have consciously done something wrong, violated a moral rule. Shame, on the other hand, is the painful feeling of lack of dignity, the impression of having a dirty soul. The worst thing for someone who is ashamed is the feeling that everyone around them sees them as unworthy and tainted.

Shame and guilt need to be treated differently. Recognizing wrongdoing, admitting it, and wanting to make reparation are enough to get rid of the normal sense of guilt. This is not the same for shame – the almost physical feeling of being soiled and disgusting. Admitting the failure or the fault is not enough to relieve the shame.

Such healing may be helped by a rite of purification, such as washing the hands or the head to dispel the sense of being tainted. Effective therapy enables the person to accept the shameful part of the self and surround it with love.

When aggression is not recognized for what it is, it is felt as anxiety.

THE PERSON WITH OBSESSIVE GUILT

Obsessive feelings of guilt are different from normal guilt feelings. Obsessive guilt feelings recur, accompanied by great anxiety. This pathological remorse continues to burden the guilty party even after the fault has been confessed, leaving the morbid need to atone, even for a minor or imagined sin. People obsessed by guilt inflict on themselves an inner torment of accusations, such as "I should have …" "Why didn't I think of that?" "It's my fault …" "It's unforgiveable …."

This obsessive feeling often masks repressed aggression, which people turn against themselves. When this aggression is not recognized for what it is, it is felt as anxiety. We find this state of mind following a sudden separation, an unexpected loss, a divorce, a heartbreak or the suicide of a close relative or friend. Children are particularly vulnerable to it because of their magical way of thinking. For example, they may think they have caused the death of someone close to them or their parents' separation through their own thoughts or actions.

THE ANXIOUS

The anxious suffer from chronic and disproportionate uneasiness towards imminent danger, which is usually imagined. Living with the sword of Damocles hanging over their heads, they predict coming catastrophes that leave them feeling a paralyzing dread. For this reason they are not inclined to take risks. Naturally pessimistic, they imagine failure, humiliation, and misfortune. Already shackled by the mere anticipation of failure, through their actions they ensure that the prophecies of doom come to pass. Their only consolation is saying, "I knew it!"

To treat people who are anxious, we must teach them to live as much as possible in the present, and to replace their fantasies of failure with ideas of success.

THE PERSON WITH CONSTANT ANGUISH

Like the anxious, the anguished live in a constant state of fear, which is as psychological as it is physical. Anguish can range from simply being preoccupied with something to full-blown panic attacks and phobias. The physical symptoms may include heavy sweating, muscle spasms, racing pulse, a feeling of suffocation, and swelling of the throat.

People with this condition do not usually understand why they feel as they do. They don't know where the anguish comes from or what it is trying to tell them. Most of the time it is their shadow in disguise. (The shadow is the repressed part of the person that tries in different ways to emerge into consciousness and there find a way to be expressed.)

As a permanent source of anguish, the shadow can become increasingly mystifying, because the person who experiences anguish is obsessed with it. Often it turns to symbolic expression, projecting itself on things, animals, and situations. Anguish thus takes on the appearance of various phobias. Some possibilities for healing are found in the integration of the shadow; some of these are found in the second part of this book.

THE DEPENDENT PERSONALITY

Dependent people are characterized by their lack of consciousness of their own psychological boundaries. Consequently, they lose themselves in their relationships with others. They become incapable of seeing and tolerating the differences that separate them from others. They use expressions of intense

Dependent people are characterized by their lack of consciousness of their own psychological boundaries.

89

In contrast with dependents and independents, people with high self-esteem have flexible psychological boundaries.

merging, such as "I know what you are going through," "You make me happy," "You're driving me crazy." Uncertain of the state of their own soul, they always feel ill at ease or threatened, either for themselves or for others.

They have low self-esteem and believe that their borders have been invaded by foreign elements. They are constantly under the influence of others, to the point of renouncing their own individuality. They have a hard time integrating the teachings and principles of their educators; they simply swallow them. They are tormented by a tyrannical superego, which can be recognized in expressions they use, such as "We should," "We must," "We must not," and in the use of "you" or "one" instead of "I."

THE INDEPENDENT PERSONALITY

People who are independent are at the opposite pole from dependents. They construct impregnable boundaries that they constantly guard to protect themselves. They always think that people are talking about them. They mistrust any show of admiration or affection; they organize things in the hope of avoiding imaginary traps so that they will receive neither admiration nor affection. They speak often of their freedom and independence, which they always believe are being threatened.

In contrast with dependents and independents, people with high self-esteem have flexible psychological boundaries. Their idea of their identity is very clear; they know what belongs to them and what does not. They know the limits of their personality and they are not defined by the opinions of others. They know how to engage with others in fulfilling relationships. They give and receive signs of attention and affection, while remaining free and independent. They allow themselves to show their vulnerability and dependence towards people whom they have chosen for their fidelity and solid friendship.

Through simple strategies, people can free themselves from these neuroses.

CONCLUSION

The description of the illnesses related to self-esteem is not very uplifting. But what is comforting is that through simple strategies, such as changing the way they see themselves, modifying their internal dialogue, and controlling their emotions and feelings, people can free themselves from these neuroses. The re-education of the self is always possible.

Part II

... to esteeming the Self

Become what you are!

— NIETZSCHE

CHAPTER 8

Moving from self-esteem to esteeming the Self

Before enlightenment, chop wood and carry water.
After enlightenment, chop wood and carry water.

— ZEN SAYING

W e need a strong self if we are going to get close to the Self, esteem it, and care for it. The first part of this book deals with developing self-esteem; this second part illustrates the importance of esteeming the Self – the soul inhabited by the divine – and the conditions that will foster this process.

Self-esteem is psychological and stems from the will; esteeming the Self is spiritual and stems from the awakening of the action of the Self.

As you read, keep in mind the distinction between self-esteem and esteeming the Self. Self-esteem has to do with the images, words, and attitudes we draw on to make value judgments about ourselves. Esteeming the Self involves discovering our soul and caring for it. Self-esteem is psychological and stems from the will; esteeming the Self is spiritual and stems from the awakening of the action of the Self. Ultimately, self-esteem is concerned with the ego, our physical, emotional, intellectual, and social survival; esteeming the Self seeks to discover our spiritual being, our soul, and to allow our soul to help us develop fully.

THE DEATH OF THE EGO
OR CONTEMPT FOR THE SELF?

Even today, many spiritual authors believe that spirituality is built on the ruins of the ego and, consequently, on contempt for the self. Because these authors are suspicious of self-esteem and healthy self-love, they concentrate on showing the potential pitfalls of self-esteem, while overlooking its benefits.

Some people equate self-esteem with such terms as narcissism, navel-gazing, individualism (as opposed to the common good), the cult of the inflated self, exaggerated concern for

Moving from self-esteem to esteeming the Self is not a result of the death of the ego, but is marked by conversion and a change of perspective.

oneself, preoccupation with the self, the self as hero, self-deification, or me first. This is unfortunate, for we must have healthy self-esteem to esteem the Self.

To move from self-esteem to esteeming the Self, some spiritual masters say we must renounce the ego — in other words, renounce self-esteem. They invite their followers to die to their self, that is, to do away with it, break it, wipe it out, make it disappear.

Being convinced of the importance of the ego or self, I am opposed to any mutilation of the self and of self-esteem. I do not understand this violent language and prefer to use more positive terms.

The elimination of the ego leads to rejection of the values that are tied to survival and to social affirmation. Moreover, such an orientation risks fuelling spiritual illusions about the self.

I wish to show that moving from self-esteem to esteeming the Self is not a result of the death of the ego, but is marked by conversion and a change of perspective. I emphasize the awakening of the self to spiritual realities. Once solid self-esteem and its survival forces are in place, I advocate a progressive change in the point of view from the ego to the transcendence of the Self. I am, in fact, convinced that spiritual growth requires the psychological well-being that healthy self-esteem fosters.

How, then, do we move from self-esteem to esteeming the Self? This shift takes place when the ego consciously renounces its central place in the person and its pretence of controlling everything, when the ego places itself under the direction of the Self.

SELF-ESTEEM AND ESTEEMING THE SELF: TWO TYPES OF GROWTH WITH OPPOSITE PROCESSES

Psychological work and spiritual work combine willpower and grace.

Michel Lacroix, a French author and university professor, makes a fine distinction between the two opposite movements involved in personal growth: the building of self-esteem, and emptying oneself of it to esteem the Self.

> On one hand, we are aiming for the reinforcement of the self: improving performance, becoming a leader, communicating better, handling our emotions, completing projects: all of this is part of affirming the self. This group of activities related to personal development affects the self. But, on the other hand, personal development envisages going beyond the self to spiritual experience.[11]

He also wrote that the ways of attaining spiritual experience are changing: "Thanks to trances, ecstasy, and widening of consciousness, subjects hope to taste cosmic fusion, to become 'people without borders,' to dissolve their individuality in the transpersonal. Such activities are clearly positioned beyond the ego."[12] Despite his excellent description of the movement from ego to Self, Lacroix falls into the trap of making the ego disappear to benefit the experience of the Self.

Following the same line of thinking, David Richo[13] parallels psychological and spiritual development. Here I borrow from his comparison between psychological work (self-esteem) and spiritual work (esteeming the Self).

Psychological work and spiritual work require the integration of these two dynamics. They combine willpower and grace. Once the efforts of intelligence and will that are part of self-esteem have been exhausted, the Self intervenes by its grace.

To make the move towards esteeming the Self, we must rely on strategies other than those used to build self-esteem — we must call on the resources of the unconscious.

There is a certain wisdom in the art of knowing the moment when we must stop trying to make things happen and open ourselves to the possibilities. To make the move towards esteeming the Self, we must rely on strategies other than those used to build self-esteem — we must call on the resources of the unconscious. These strategies consist of putting ourselves in another state, notably by self-hypnosis, meditation, visualization or affirmation and, above all, showing that we are open to the energies and the symbols of the Self. These promote the action of the Self, which harbours possibilities for growth that the ego does not have.

Thus, Jung affirmed: "Growth of the personality comes through the unconscious."[14] This view corresponds to that of Milton Erickson. This great hypnotherapist, who influenced most modern schools of psychotherapy, saw the unconscious as the place where all possible growth could take place, because it is an inexhaustible source of creativity.

MOVING FROM THE LIFE OF THE EGO TO THE SPIRITUAL LIFE

No one can predict exactly how a particular individual will move from the life of the ego to that of the Self, but we can identify three major categories of people who make this passage.

1. Some people, from their youth, are attuned to the urgings of the Self and follow them gently.

2. Others, particularly at mid-life, live through an existential crisis. Even though they have material and social success and ought to be on top of the world, they are haunted by existential questions and reflections: "What's it all about?" "What is the meaning of my life?" "I have the feeling that I've messed up my

life, that I went in the wrong direction." "I feel utterly alone, even though I'm surrounded by people who care about me."

3. Others ask themselves these existential questions following major losses in their life.

For those in the last two groups, the movement from self-esteem to esteeming the Self is not easy. Their spiritual awakening goes through periods of anguish. If they are not guided and warned, they quickly become discouraged and return to their boring routine and superficial diversions. But if they remain faithful to the urgings of the Self, they will learn how to face these difficult moments and will progress on their spiritual path.

The discovery of the Self's influences on the ego can cause existential fear.

THE EXPERIENCE OF ANGUISH IN SPIRITUAL GROWTH

The discovery of the Self's influences on the ego can cause existential fear. Unfortunately, few works describe this anguish. The word *anguish* comes from the Latin *angustia*, which means *narrow passage*. It hearkens back to the typical suffocating sensation felt in the throat and in the chest, which makes a person feel "closed in" because of an energy blockage.

The conversion from self-esteem to esteeming the Self — that is, the self sacrificing itself for the sake of the Self — arouses a particular kind of anguish. This fear is born of the self's mourning for its security and the vertigo it feels before the unfamiliar spiritual world. (It is important, however, to not confuse this type of anguish with the anguish caused by repression.) It wells up when the Self prompts a growth spurt; paradoxically, it is accompanied by a sense of enthusiasm. Furthermore, it signals a crisis. The ego is worried because it no longer feels secure;

The mourning for old securities that the self must undergo results in a strange sense of newness, even emptiness.

it loses its stability and can no longer control its development. In short, it no longer knows what the future holds.

The mourning for old securities that the self must undergo results in a strange sense of newness, even emptiness. But rather than face up to this discomfort and confusion bravely, people often tend to turn to the comfort of the self. They think they have made a wrong turn, mistakenly believing that their spiritual evolution should happen easily and painlessly. Wise is the spiritual companion who can identify these fleeting obstacles because she has gone through them herself, and has known these "dark nights of the soul." She is in a position to support novices on the arid path of spiritual progress.

THE PHENOMENON OF INDUCTION

Induction is another form of anguish rarely recognized at the beginning of spiritual awakening and the radiance of the Self. This term, borrowed from physics, describes the resistance that an electric current undergoes when it travels through a metal conductor that heats up and even burns. This metaphor is used in spiritual psychology to describe the energized radiance of the Self when it begins to enlighten obscure areas of the unconscious. It discloses instances of immaturity, youthful follies, moral transgressions, and giving up on our ideals. The Self thus encounters strong resistance in the form of anguish.

The phenomenon of induction appears more clearly when someone commits themselves to living high spiritual ideals: a young novice in a religious order is drawn to a great ideal, but lacks self-confidence; early in his marriage, a man feels imprisoned by his commitment; after the birth of her child, a mother experiences a deep sense of guilt about a past abortion; someone who has vowed to live an ideal of perfect chastity is obsessed by sexual images; a religious community that was originally passionate about saving the world focuses on its own concerns instead. If the spiritual ideal is lived only in the realm of thought, induction will probably not be set in motion. On the other hand, if people decide to live the ideal concretely, induction will likely be activated.

Two paths enable people to esteem the Self: the negative path and the positive path.

In the same line of thought, Robert Johnson[15] has noted that the shadow re-emerges and tends to appear after an intense spiritual period. Similarly, Aldous Huxley, in *Devils of Loudun*, also indicates the polarization that results from induction: "Each positive engenders a corresponding negative ... we discover things like hate that accompanies love, derision caused by respect and admiration."[16]

Someone who has become more sensitive to spiritual values and, at the same time, more responsible, will be more likely to feel guilt and a healthy shame when facing certain attitudes and actions from their past. If, instead of repressing this guilt and shame, they accept them and reintegrate them as they would their shadow, their self will experience an astonishing expansion of consciousness and sense a surprising truth. But, once again, for this to happen, they must be accompanied by an attentive spiritual master who will not downplay the experience of induction.

TWO PATHS TO ESTEEMING THE SELF

Two paths enable people to esteem the Self: the negative path and the positive path. In contrast to self-esteem, which grows as a result of effort, practice, and strategies, esteeming the Self happens very differently.

Before we go further, we will define more precisely the psychospiritual authority of the Self.

The negative way entails a purification through the following strategies: disidentification, mourning, integration of the shadow, and voluntary detachment.

The positive or symbolic path uses other strategies: work on symbols using the active imagination, the practice of the mandala, study of the symbolism of dreams, reconciling of opposites, and knowledge of spiritual myths and stories.

Chapters 12 and 13 will describe both types of strategies in detail. But before we go further, we will define more precisely the psychospiritual authority of the Self.

CHAPTER 9

What is the Self?

I knew that I had attained, through the mandala,
the expression of the Self,
the ultimate discovery that I have been permitted to make.

— CARL JUNG

JUNG'S UNDERSTANDING OF THE SELF

Carl Jung discovered the authority of the Self by analyzing his own dreams and those of his patients; by doing anthropological research, particularly into Tibetan mandalas; and by studying alchemy, taoism, and Gnosticism. His studies led him to discover evidence of the existence of a centre of the soul, the organizing principle of the whole person. He borrowed from India the word *atman*, which means *self* or *oneself*. In the ancient Vedic texts, the Upanishads use this term to designate the true person, as opposed to a self that is considered an artificial covering, a random crystallization. For Élie Humbert, this intuition is "the keystone of Jungian psychology."[17]

Jung distanced himself from the theory of his own teacher, Freud. He no longer accepted Freud's concept of the unconscious, the Freudian "id" driven only by chaotic libidinal forces that can break into consciousness at any moment and produce a psychosis. The Jungian unconscious is less menacing. It is made up of archetypes, bundles of psychic energy that are enfleshed in reality to give it meaning. Ideally, these universal forms gravitate around a centre that is the Self. Along with the Self, which Jung calls "the royal archetype," these archetypes form the collective unconscious.

So while Freud asks that the self adopt a defensive attitude towards the unconscious, and commands the self to build defences to contain the unconscious, Jung proposes collabora-

Carl Jung's studies led him to discover evidence of the existence of a centre of the soul, the organizing principle of the whole person.

Jung proposes an original understanding of the inner life.

tion between the conscious and unconscious self. Freud's concept of the unconscious is purely of the psychological order, and is closed to any openness to the spiritual. In Jung's thought, the collective unconscious is organized around a religious and spiritual centre, the Self, which he defines as the *imago Dei* (image of God). In 1930, Jung came to the conclusion that the collective unconscious is centred on the authority of the Self, which gives meaning and purpose to all psychic material. The discovery of the Self led him to conceive of a process of maturation of the person whose goal is to become "oneSelf," to rediscover his or her real identity (or individuality) and, to this end, free the person from alienating social influences.

By attributing to the Self such status – as both the totality and the finality of psychic life – Jung proposes an original understanding of the inner life. It would no longer be a simple psychological activity, but a spirituality of the Self. Because of his theories, all the schools of transpersonal psychology now recognize the determining role of the spiritual in the evolution of the person.

INTUITIVE KNOWLEDGE OF THE SELF

We come to know the Self not by direct experience, but by hints that reveal its presence. We know it only through peak experiences in which the Self breaks through. These allow us to glimpse the Self in the course of ordinary life. Among these peak experiences – which I will discuss at length in the next chapter – I will focus here on those of a more symbolic character.

The Self, which is a reality that cannot be known directly, can be discovered by the conscious through symbols: dreams, myths, and legends. Among the symbolic images that represent the Self more particularly, we put at the top of the list those that represent totality and infinity, such as a priceless gem, an indestructible diamond, pure gold, living water, a phoenix rising from the ashes, the fountain of youth, the philosopher's stone, the inner kingdom. Next we examine images that lead us to a centre surrounded by infinite space, such as the mandala, the cross, the North Star, the cubes and the circle. Each of these symbols refers us back to the idea of totality, of perfection, of the purpose of the Self, the human soul inhabited by the divine.

"The Self is the imago Dei (image of God), the 'God in us.'"

ATTEMPTS TO DESCRIBE THE SELF

What is the Self? Jung offers several responses to this question: "The Self is the royal archetype of the whole person; the Self is the totality and purpose of the psyche; the Self is the *imago Dei* (image of God), the 'God in us.'"[18]

Edward C. Whitmont defines it as an autonomous inner personality, different from the conscious self. He considers it to be a guide that promotes the unfolding and orientation of the ego.[19]

John Firman also sees the Self as different from the "conscious I," but in relationship with it. He affirms the influence of the Self as much on the interior as on the exterior of the "I." "The Self is the deeper ontological reality of which the 'I' is a reflection," says Firman.[20]

The hypnotherapist Stephen Gilligan offers a more poetic definition that helps us understand the nature and role of the Self:

> The soul is a sanctuary in the inner self where a fresh waterfall always runs deep in a tropical forest, a harbour of calm and serenity under whose branches lives a very wise man. This man has lived from the begin-

The Self is immanent in all the physical, mental, and spiritual aspects of the human person.

ning of time. He is not an old man, not at all. Rather let us say that he is ageless. He knows how to live. He knows what is good for him. He does not deceive himself. He knows how to derive great pleasure from life, to draw lessons from it, and acquire strength and power from them. He is the centre of the generative Self.[21]

To conclude, we can compare the Jungian Self to Plato's understanding of the soul. The soul is inhabited by fantastic shadows from the cave (the archetypes of meaning) and shares in the divine life. The Self in Carl Jung's thought is also the human soul in which the divine resides.

THE CHARACTERISTICS OF THE SELF

The Self programs the whole person

Some people tend to make of the Self a purely spiritual reality that tyrannically dominates the body and the emotions. On the contrary, the Self is immanent in all the physical, mental, and spiritual aspects of the human person. Like DNA controls our genetic development, the Self controls the development and the evolution of the whole person, body and psyche, at the same time. Whitmont comments, "We find it continually attuned, continually responding, reacting and spontaneously initiating new developments which appear *as if* planned for a specific individual, even though arising and functioning regardless of, and at times contrary to, this person's conscious ideas, wishes and intentions."[22]

The Self reveals itself as transcendent, since it goes beyond the confines of the person whose interactions with the outside world it manages. John Firman agrees: "The transcendent-

immanent Self is the most profound Being, the universal personal 'I am who am.' "[23] Thus it avoids the Cartesian dualism that
would make the body and soul distinct, juxtaposed substances,
not interpenetrating ones. In short, the Self oversees a number
of organic biological, mental, and spiritual centres, in addition
to controlling the person's concept of the universe.

Jung insists less on the body-soul unity of the Self and
focuses instead on the psychic unity of the conscious and
unconscious: "As you know, I have defined the Self as the totality of the conscious and unconscious psyche."[24]

To clarify the relationship of the Self to the conscious
psyche, we could say that the Self and the conscious psyche are
complementary. The Self's role is to correct and fill out the conscious content or the attitudes of the self-persona. For example,
if someone is too nice or too obsequious with their domineering boss, the Self will have them dream that their boss is a
tyrant and the dreamer will behave in a servile manner towards
him. The dream will condemn what has not been recognized in
the employee-employer relationship. Jung observed, "The only
functional meaning of the Self is when it can act to compensate
the consciousness of the self."[25] In short, the Self is responsible
for re-establishing balance when the ego behaves excessively.

The Self and the conscious psyche are complementary.

The Self: central organizing principle

The Self is a vaster, more important control centre than
the conscious ego. Often people believe, mistakenly, that the ego
and its persona form the essential part of the personality; they
do not recognize that there is a higher authority, the Self, that
determines the evolution of the ego. The discovery of the Self
was as fundamental and important to the field of psychology as
the Copernican revolution that shifted the centre of the universe
from the earth to the sun was to science. In affirming this central

The Self acts as a unifying energy field that engages inner and outer worlds at the same time.

place of the Self, Jung banished the common belief that had established the conscious ego as the primary decision-making centre of the person. The conscious ego is nothing but a satellite of the Self, which created and manages it.

Edward Whitmont grants the Self a key role in the evolution of the person: "The *modus operandi* of the Self may be likened to the centre of an energy field which aims towards fulfilling a life and personality pattern which as a potentiality is *a priori* given."[26]

It can be compared to the North Star, by which sailors chart their course but never reach.[27]

The timeless Self

The Self is timeless; it never ages. Because of its constant newness, it possesses as many characteristics of youth as of wise old age. Thus it is equally well represented by the archetype of the eternal child (*puer aeternus*) as by that of the wise elder.

To the Self belongs the mythical time that lasts as long as eternity, not linear time of the past, present, and future. Like the current of a river, it is an eternal present. One moment of linear time would be like a bucket of water filled from the same river.

Synchronicity and the Self

The synchronicity of the Self refers to the mysterious agreement between the psyche and the outside world. A person's psychic activity is not limited to intellectual activity. The Self acts as a unifying energy field that engages inner and outer worlds at the same time. For example, a writer who is overly rational asks himself how to improve his writing style. He receives the response to his question in a message from the universe: in his travels he encounters some kind-hearted women, and comes to understand that he should tap into his feminine sensitivity and emotional side more fully. The Self's synchronicity does not observe linear time or cause and effect, but transcends the temporal categories of past, present, and future.

Jung liked to tell a story about this phenomenon. One day, he was analyzing the dream of one of his female clients, in which she had received the gift of a beetle. He writes: "While she was telling me about her dream, I saw an insect flying by hit the window [...], it provided the closest analogy that we can possibly find to a gold beetle in our part of the world: it was a large, slow-moving beetle."[28] Jung saw a striking connection between his client's dream and the sudden appearance of the insect. He argued that there is a "meaningful coincidence" between psychic work and reality. To him, both beetles appeared as a symbol foreshadowing his client's rebirth.

The Self that Jung defined as "the image of God" is neither male nor female.

The androgynous Self

The Self that Jung defined as "the image of God" is neither male nor female. This image of God to which he refers takes us back to the text of Genesis: "God created man in his image, male and female he created them" (Genesis 1.27). This phrase indicates that God has no gender, but is the harmonious synthesis of masculine and feminine attributes.

Thus the Self has an androgynous character. Whoever desires communion with the Self should strive for it by developing equally both the traits of their own gender and those of the opposite gender. Men must integrate their *anima* (their inner female), and women, their *animus* (their inner male).

The healing Self

We have seen that the Self plays the role of the central organizing principle of the whole person. Its job is to integrate and harmonize all dimensions of the person.

The Self represents a paradox: it represents on one hand the hidden real and true being that needs liberation and, on the other hand, the link with the universe.

Jung explains most neuroses and psychoses as a lack of co-ordination between the conscious orientations of the self and the unconscious orientations of the Self. The Self takes responsibility for establishing inner harmony or for re-establishing it when it has become unbalanced. This is its healing role.

More concretely, therapists argue that if their clients cannot reach a consciously desired goal, it is because of unconscious resistances. Therefore, if someone wants to stop smoking or lose weight, unconscious blockages can prevent them from meeting their objectives. If conscious and unconscious goals are out of balance, the Self's role is to reconcile them by creating integrating symbols that re-establish harmony between the fragmented parts of a person's being.

Jung defines the healing Self thus: "It is a perfect *coincidentia oppositorum* [meeting of opposites] that expresses its divine nature." The Self intervenes, for example, when tensions and conflicts arise. "Psychological experience shows that symbols of the Self surface in dreams and in the active imagination when opposing points of view clash most violently."[29]

In workshops on the shadow of the personality, I have often experienced the healing power of the Self. When opposing symbols are at work,[30] I ask participants to seek the integrating power of their Self. I am always astonished by the richness of the symbols that result from this exercise. In many people, these symbols manifest a sacred, luminous character as well as bring healing.

The Self in relationship to the universe

The Self represents a paradox: it represents on one hand the hidden real and true being that needs liberation and, on the other hand, the link with the universe. It stands for individuality in its uniqueness even as it links this individuality to the collective unconscious. The fulfillment of the Self, "becoming oneself," accomplishes what is most personal and original in the self, even while it reflects and, indeed, embraces, the universe. As Jung says, "The Self embraces infinitely more in itself than simply the self, as symbolism has always shown. It is as much the other and the others as me. Individuation does not exclude the world, but includes it."[31]

The Self has a living connection with nature.

In this instance, the Self participates mystically with the universe. Who has not experienced an intimate communion with the outer world, even with inanimate things, during privileged moments? The poet Lamartine describes this experience in two celebrated lines:

Inanimate things, have you then a soul
that attaches itself to mine and forces it to love?[32]

The Self also enables us to have "animist" attitudes towards nature, the polar opposite of the rational and technical approach that tries to master nature. The Self is more interested in collaborating with nature, of becoming a co-creator, than controlling it. People discover more and more that the Self has a living connection with nature. Modern ecology is attempting to rediscover this vital link.

When he was old, Jung shared this confidence: "At times, it is as though I am spread throughout the countryside and in things, and I saw myself in every tree, in the lapping of the waves, in the clouds, in the animals that come and go, and in objects ... Here there is a place for the realm of backgrounds situated outside of space."[33]

CHAPTER 10

The relationships between the ego and the Self

THE OLD SELF THAT CANNOT BE UPROOTED

*O*nce upon a time a monk was determined to destroy his ego
in order to wipe out any trace of vanity or self-love. He
therefore decided to dress like a poor man, never to speak of
himself, never to let any attachments develop, to avoid all originality
and to possess nothing that could set him apart from others.

He was constantly on the lookout for the least sign of pride or
vanity in himself. He became angry with himself when he felt proud to
be wearing clean clothes. He came up with all kinds of tactics to deflect
the slightest interest in himself, and refused all compliments. He forced
distractions on himself so he wouldn't think of himself. He had almost
succeeded in eliminating his ego.

During his frequent examinations of conscience, he caught
himself admiring his poverty and comparing his self-emptying with that
of others.

He thus found that he was too attached to his detachment and to
his external appearance of holiness.

He became more and more stressed by his fruitless efforts to kill
his ego. His personality changed: he became more and more irritable;
he often lacked charity towards his brothers. This caused him great
humiliation.

Finally, completely drained, he decided to act like everyone else:
he dressed appropriately, ate, accepted compliments, talked about himself
like the other monks did.

Instead of desperately trying to eradicate his ego, he set about
loving himself.

Authentically esteeming the Self can only build on solid self-esteem, that is, on a self that esteems itself highly.

IS THE DEATH OF THE EGO ESSENTIAL FOR ESTEEMING THE SELF?

In order to esteem the Self, must we give up self-esteem? Certain spiritual writers tend to consider self-esteem as an obstacle to the spiritual life and its growth. They present "the death of the ego," "the dissolution of the self," "the absence of the self" or "dying to self" as a spiritual ideal to be pursued. Such murderous expressions do grave harm to an individual's psychological and spiritual growth. In addition, they create the illusion that we can master ourselves perfectly and contribute to spiritual pride.

In a workshop on spirituality in which I was participating, the facilitator engaged us in a ritual designed to put our ego to death. At the end of the ritual, the psychologists in the groups indicated the danger of such an exercise, particularly for immature participants who already lacked self-esteem. These people could hardly put their self-esteem to death when they had almost none!

Authentically esteeming the Self can only build on solid self-esteem, that is, on a self that esteems itself highly. Without this, people are destined to remain spiritually immature and filled with illusions.

THE EGO, A REFLECTION OF THE SELF

How can we define the relationship between the ego and the Self? John Firman attempts to do this in his book *I and Self: Revisioning Psychosynthesis*. He rejects the idea of making the ego an extension of the Self, like a branch of a tree or a stream whose source is a lake. Rather, he looks at the ego as an image of the Self. The Self is the flame that is reflected in a mirror; the ego is the reflection or image of the flame. The reflection owes its existence to the flame. To the extent that the reflection is not distorted, it will faithfully represent the real flame; it will almost be identified with it.

The same is true of the ego. To the extent that it recognizes its dependence on the Self and obeys its orientations, the ego will resemble it more and more closely, to the point of becoming its faithful reflection. It will identify increasingly with the Self. But if the ego denies its dependence on the Self, through either ignorance or pride-filled vanity (hubris), it distances itself from its living source, and will no longer assimilate itself to the Self. The ego will go so far as to consider itself, mistakenly, as the centre of psychological life, even though it moves within the orbit of the Self. No longer will it be anything except a deformed image of the Self. Dissociated from its creative source, the ego will end up alienated from the Self. Inevitably, it will lose the sense of its own existence and lock itself into a pathology that can progress from neurosis to psychosis.

A METAPHOR FOR THE RELATIONSHIPS BETWEEN THE EGO AND THE SELF

Most people misunderstand the role of the ego, seeing it as the centre of their personality that is busy directing their lives. A popular saying presents the ego as all-powerful will: "When you want to, you can." If they fail to free themselves from a dependence on cigarettes, food or alcohol, for example, these people recognize that this saying expresses a half-truth.

Edward Whitmont offers an enlightening allegory on the relationship between the ego and the Self.[34] He compares the ego to a mayor who, to his great surprise, discovers in his city the existence of an authority above his own. He feels overcome by this revelation. From now on he must submit himself to the

Most people misunderstand the role of the ego, seeing it as the centre of their personality that is busy directing their lives.

According to Jung, the ego depends on the Self, from which it draws both its substance and its growth.

orders of a mysterious central power that speaks in a different language and is situated far away — say in central Asia or on Mars. He is even more upset to learn that a local militia, independent of the city police, obeys the law and orders dictated by this higher authority. This situation worries him greatly and seriously disrupts the management of his city.

Who is this mysterious authority? What is this central power that rules the whole territory? It is the Self.

We are led to believe that the ego or conscious self is master of all psychic activity. This is untrue! According to Jung, the ego depends on the Self, from which it draws both its substance and its growth. It is not the "I" that creates me, but the Self that constructs me. Thus with a certain anguish the ego, even as it remains itself, must give way to the Self, as we have seen above.

THE IMPORTANCE OF THE EGO'S DIALOGUE WITH THE SELF

The ego, therefore, must engage constantly with the symbolic revelations that the Self transmits through dreams and peak experiences, however confused and unsettling they may seem. If the conscious "I" trusts the Self and its symbolic messages, the "I" will flourish more readily because it is plugged into its spiritual source. The healthy effects that the ego will draw from such an exchange include the ability to accept and love unconditionally; the experience of a deep harmony within itself and with the Universe; the acquisition of wisdom; the ability to heal itself; and the discovery of the personal mission that the Universe offers.

REALIGNING THE EGO AND THE SELF

We must not believe that the ego is concerned only with the survival of our body and our psychic life, and that the Self is confined to spiritual aspects. This would be a dualistic concept of the Self. The Self permeates and influences every aspect of the ego and all its activities. It is simultaneously both immanent and transcendent (see pages 107–108, The Self: central organizing principle).

To illustrate how the ego and the Self are intertwined, I will use a map of human experience borrowed from neurolinguistic programming, notably from the philosopher Gregory Bateson. The map describes the logical levels of learning appropriate to the ego and the Self. We will use here both the description and the coordinates.

The domain of the ego

Under the Self's influence, the ego exerts its power on the following levels of learning.

Environment

The ego is free to choose its surroundings: for example, clothing, physical environment, home décor, social class, temperature, atmosphere, and so on.

Behaviours

It controls the following behaviours: the elegance of gestures, upright posture, physical balance, breathing, step, the know-how to live in society, ability to relax, and so on.

Skills employed with the help of strategies

In neurolinguistic programming, the ego manages mental skills and the organization of external and internal systems of

The Self permeates and influences every aspect of the ego and all its activities.

Someone's ego thus can put in place effective strategies.

representation: that is, visual (V), auditory (A), kinesthetic (K), olefactory (O), and gustatory (G).

A strategy is a way of organizing systems of representation to accomplish a task successfully. For example, to use an excellent method of spelling, a person must first be able to visualize the word in their head (V), sound it out quietly (A), and emotionally verify it so that he or she has the feeling that they have succeeded in spelling it correctly. Other strategies exist for carrying out these tasks with excellence.

Counting on its tendency to esteem itself, and with the help of appropriate exercises, the ego will use the external senses and try to develop their acuity: sight, sound, touch, taste, and smell. It has the ability to constantly refine conscience and the development of internal perceptions: for example, the variety and richness of its images, the quality of internal dialogues, a more lively consciousness of emotions and a greater ability to express them.

Someone's ego thus can put in place effective strategies, which I presented in the first part of this book. We will list them again here:

- Everyone can succeed in appreciating themselves as persons if they
  - see themselves as loved and lovable;
  - tell themselves that they are loved and lovable;
  - feel that they are loved and lovable; and
  - work at undoing their false perceptions of themselves and replacing them with healthy perceptions.
- They will be able to accomplish certain tasks or projects if they
  - see themselves succeed;
  - tell themselves that they are capable;

- feel confident; and
- work at undoing their false conceptions of themselves that harm their ability to act and replacing them with more appropriate and effective conceptions.
• In loving themselves and trusting their own competence, they will be able to work at affirming themselves.

The Self preserves a person's identity by reorganizing and reuniting their sub-personalities, the parts of which they are composed.

Beliefs and values

The ego also has the capacity to evaluate acquired beliefs about itself, others, and life in general. In addition it has the capacity to replace harmful or limiting beliefs with more expansive beliefs about itself, others, and life. For example, someone who believes that they will never amount to anything can transform this conviction by telling themselves, "I was born for happiness and success."

The domain of the Self

The Self: responsible for safeguarding a person's identity

The Self preserves a person's identity by reorganizing and reuniting their sub-personalities, the parts of which they are composed. The Self is particularly concerned with the reintegration of the person's shadow, those unloved parts that the person has repressed in the unconscious and projected onto others.

The manifestations of the Self, as we have seen, take the form of symbols, including integrating symbols. These symbols are responsible for rebuilding and harmonizing the fragmented, scattered parts of the personality.

119

The ego has no choice but to follow the direction of the Self if it does not want to wither away.

The Self: a creator of spiritual experiences

The Self, which we have identified with "the soul inhabited by the divine" or with "the image of the divine in the self," may be discovered in peak experiences that are often symbolic. Among other things, these eruptions of the Self in the field of consciousness are revealed by:

- the feeling of being loved unconditionally;
- the search for a wisdom that gives meaning to life and death;
- the healing of illnesses that lead to reconciliation and the harmonization of conflictual elements in the personality; and
- the discovery of our personal mission.

CONCLUSION

Many people do not know that the Self exists in them, and so live at the level of the ego. Although the ego thinks it is the master of the person, the Self is subtly leading the ego. The ego has an important role to play, but it is always under the direction of the Self. When the ego overlooks or even rebels against the orientations of the Self, there is imbalance and the danger that physical, psychological or spiritual illnesses will develop. The ego has no choice but to follow the direction of the Self if it does not want to wither away.

CHAPTER II

Looking beyond the ego to the Self

The Self is nothing more than this "beyond the self,"
this yearning to be that is never fully realized,
although it is constantly drawn, as by a magnet,
towards completion.

— YSÉ TARDAN-MASQUELIER

The passage from self-esteem to esteeming the Self — that is, from the ego to the Self — is a work of collaboration, not conflict. Esteeming the Self is not built on the destruction of self-esteem; rather, there is a continuity between the two realities. Once the ego has acquired values, the Self must direct them. How can we help this transition happen?

I do not have space here to make an exhaustive list of all the changes of attitude that result when the influence of the ego gives way to that of the Self, but I will note a few of them. My aim is to explore the transformation that takes place when the ego makes way for the Self, especially in terms of the inner being, social relationships, and links with the Universe.

The spiritual life consists of always exploring more deeply the inner life as it emerges.

INNER MANIFESTATIONS OF ESTEEMING THE SELF

Esteeming the Self and the conversion to the inner life

For me, the spiritual journey consists of returning to the beginning of ourselves, that is, to the experience of Being.

— RICHARD MOSS

The spiritual life consists of always exploring more deeply the inner life as it emerges: images, daydreams, dreams, creative visions, inner dialogues, and emotions and feelings. It is not easy to turn inwards and let the flood of images, words, and

Meditation is the principal means of fostering the awakening of consciousness about our inner world.

emotions invade us and shake us up. Most people prefer to stay outside themselves. Instead of welcoming these inner messages, they distract themselves with entertainment and constant activity. They contrive to silence the states of the soul that go against their habits or desires. As Henri Le Saux has affirmed, "To be wise is to gather oneself up again and focus on the place from which everything springs forth. This is the holiest act; this is love, this is wisdom, this is union."[35]

Meditation is the principal means of fostering the awakening of consciousness about our inner world. To keep attention fixed on the inner self, meditation relies on consciousness of the rhythms of the breath or the repetition of a mantra or word. Next, it allows the flood of words, images, and emotions to come to consciousness. They are allowed to float by, like clouds observed in a blue sky. In this way we learn to distance ourselves from these inner phenomena and prevent them from having too firm a hold over us. Thus we can develop the capacity to enter into an attitude of inner detachment, which gives us greater freedom. This is the practice described in the Yoga sutra: "By observing the movement of the breath, its depth or shallowness and its rhythm, we come to a subtle, long breath. Then what is hiding the light is broken up, and the spirit becomes able to focus."[36]

Esteeming the Self and peak experiences

The ego is satisfied with the daily grind, the physical necessities of life and habits. It lives at the level of ordinary consciousness that spiritual masters compare with lethargy or sleep. Peak experiences, when the Self breaks in, wake up the ego suddenly. These experiences are not to be taken lightly; there is nothing ordinary about them.

We cannot prepare for a peak experience. It happens unexpectedly when we're looking for something, questioning, when we experience a physical shock or a huge psychological emptiness.

Abraham Maslow was one of the first to take a scientific interest in peak experiences. He undertook a survey of this phenomenon with 190 students, of whom he asked the following question: "I would like to know what you think of the most marvelous experience of your life: a moment of happiness, of ecstasy, of rapture; you might have experienced this when you were in love, or while listening to music, or when you were suddenly fascinated by a book or a painting, or even during a period of creation."[37] In each instance, these were experiences of sudden and exceptional awe and incredible joy, of unexpected happiness, of immense, uncontrollable and transcendent emotions beyond the ego's reach. Maslow concluded his research with the following reflection: "Every individual who at a given moment undergoes an intense experience has temporarily the characteristics that I have encountered in personalities who are in the process of self-actualization."[38]

At the heart of a peak experience, people experience a feeling that is different from a simple perception, idea or fleeting emotion.

At the heart of a peak experience, people experience a feeling that is different from a simple perception, idea or fleeting emotion. Such a feeling creates communion with the object and a sensation of the infinite. They are in contact with a transcendent reality: love, light, beauty or existence, for example.

These unforeseen experiences are more frequent than we might believe. David Hay and Kate Hunt draw attention to the astonishing existence of spiritual experiences in Great Britain.[39] A survey by the British Broadcasting Corporation showed that more than 76 per cent of the population reported having had a spiritual and religious experience. Unfortunately, most of these

When we discover within ourselves an unintegrated shadow, we should abandon ourselves to the integrating energy of the Self.

people are not conscious of having lived peak experiences and do not tap into the resources that would enable them to live better and to grow.

Esteeming the Self and spiritual letting go

People need to tap into the spiritual energy of the Self at certain times in their lives, especially when they seek healing. There is great wisdom in being able to know when to act intentionally and when to let the energy of the Self take over.

Two obsessions (among many) that the deliberate efforts of the ego are unable to resolve are addiction and the work of the shadow. Using the will to overcome dependency on alcohol, drugs, cigarettes or food will prove useless if we do not abandon ourselves to the spiritual energy of the Self. The philosophy of Alcoholics Anonymous justly holds that in order to stop dependence on alcohol, people must give themselves over to a spiritual power that is bigger than the ego. In doing so we can be liberated from our enslavements.

In the same way, when we discover within ourselves an unintegrated shadow, we should abandon ourselves to the integrating energy of the Self. Suppose that I experience a real antipathy towards a particular person. If I find that person is very aggressive towards me, it is because I unduly exaggerate this trait. My exaggeration indicates that I am unconsciously projecting onto this person my own aggression, which I am always trying to repress. I am not conscious that this is about my own aggression projected onto the other person. It is as though I am seeing my own aggression in a mirror; I hate it because it contradicts the extreme gentleness that those around me like so much in me and that I've gone to a lot of trouble to cultivate in myself. If I can recognize that my vision was a bit shaken by this projection, I tell myself, "Why, then, am I giving so much importance to this aggressive person? Why am I constantly obsessing about them?"

Fortunately, if I become conscious that it's my own repressed aggression, my shadow, that is reflecting on the other, I will have no other choice than to appeal to the Self to reintegrate it. Only the Self, with its unifying energy, is able to unite my extreme gentleness and my repressed aggression. Once this reintegration has taken place, I will be able to use both my gentleness and my aggression appropriately.

Self-esteem and finding our mission

My book *How to Discover Your Personal Mission* distinguishes mission from work or a job. Mission is much bigger than what we do for a living. In a job, the ego tries to deal with the necessities of life and to make a place in society. The Self, however, encourages us to adopt our personal mission; it inspires the dream of our soul, which is defined by a profound passion for a specific activity undertaken for the good of the community.

Sometimes people find themselves faced with an alternative: a job or their mission. Choosing your mission, the path that will fulfill your deepest desires, often involves giving up certain material advantages that go with a good job: fame, prestige, wealth, security, comfort, immediate satisfaction. But these sacrifices are easy to make if the trade off is the chance to fulfill ourselves through ongoing enthusiasm in our mission. The ideal situation would, of course, be to find an activity that allows us both to accomplish our mission and earn a living. Many people find a happy compromise, supporting themselves with a job and living their mission in a variety of other ways.

The Self encourages us to adopt our personal mission; it inspires the dream of our soul.

From the complexity of the ego to the unity and harmony of the Self

When thousands of things are seen in their unity,
we return to the origins,
and we stay where we have always lived.

— Zen Master Sengstan

The conscious ego is often plagued by conflicting emotions (I love and I hate at the same time), incompatible desires (I want adventure, but I like my comfort), opposing attitudes (I want to be compassionate towards strangers, but I'm suspicious of them), and goals that my behaviours contradict (I want to lose weight and stop smoking, but I am not willing to cut back).

The ego is unable to find a solution to these apparent contradictions and conflicts. It must accept the help of a higher power, the Self, which will resolve these conflicts. The global vision of the Self and its unifying power will succeed in making complementary elements out of the ego's fragments. The Self will find a reconciling symbol between the complexes that destroy the unity of the ego. This is the function of *reconciliatio oppositorum* (the reconciliation of opposites), the master-function of the Self in the processes of individuation or of becoming fully mySelf.

We will return to the idea of the fragmented ego, outlining the technique designed to harmonize the opposing parts.

Esteeming the Self and eliminating fear

Do not fear either poverty,
or exile or prison or death.
Rather, fear fear.

— Epicletus

The Self lives outside of time; it is in touch with unchanging realities, such as the creative intelligence of the Universe.

"To become spiritual is to progressively eliminate our fears," said a wise master to his disciples. The ego constantly lives in fear: fear of not being accepted, appreciated, admired or loved, for example. Its greatest terror is death. The Self, meanwhile, lives outside of time; it is in touch with unchanging realities, such as the creative intelligence of the Universe. It enjoys a vision of life beyond death. It goes through life without flinching before adversity and even the certitude of death.

While the ego panics at the thought of death, the Self is reassured because it knows how to die and is ready for another life. This is the conclusion Jung's disciple Marie-Louise von Franz drew from her studies of the dreams of people with terminal illnesses. Their dreams, which come from their Self, contained symbols of rebirth. Their unconscious was telling them that there is life beyond death.[40]

Esteeming the Self and gaining greater autonomy

The less the individual's ego is subjected to others' scrutiny, approval or admiration, the more it becomes autonomous and entrusts itself to the wisdom of the Self. Little by little it liberates itself from the constraints of social and financial status, from the opinion of those around it and of its culture. Freed from the dictates imposed by a context and concern for style and advertising, it allows itself to be guided more readily by the intuitions and orientations of the Self.

When people move from self-esteem to esteeming the Self, the change in their behaviour is dramatic.

INDICATORS OF ESTEEMING THE SELF IN HUMAN RELATIONSHIPS

Begin with the self, but do not end with the self;
take oneself for the point of departure, but not for the destination;
know oneself, but do not be preoccupied with oneself.

— MARTIN BUBER

In my practice, I have observed the positive social effects of esteeming the Self: unconditional love of self and others, inner healing, wisdom, and a mission oriented towards the community.

When people move from self-esteem to esteeming the Self, the change in their behaviour is dramatic.

Under the impetus of the Self, they are less fearful, more secure, less defensive. They are more daring, letting themselves be known in their true light; they are less afraid of revealing their vulnerability in human relationships, particularly with their friends. They foster intimacy without being afraid to expose their own inner life and even their weaknesses.

They are more open to receiving gratefully than to giving; even though they have become generous, they do not use their generosity to control others.

They no longer feel the need to compare themselves with others; they are more themselves in human relationships. Because they have become less competitive, they take an interest in others out of real solidarity.

Above all, they seek life-giving relationships; they avoid maintaining useful and worldly relationships for the sake of gaining recognition, adulation or favours.

They lose their desire for judging others by subjective criteria, and refrain from condemning them because they are

conscious that they do not know their full intentions and motivations.

Finally, esteeming the Self, which brings inner healing and
a surplus of love to the person, will be the source of compassion
and forgiveness for one's self and others.

*Those who esteem
the Self entrust
themselves to
a universal
Intelligence.*

SIGNS OF ESTEEMING THE SELF
IN RELATIONSHIPS WITH THE UNIVERSE

Prayer begins when power ends.

— RABBI ABRAHAM HESCHEL

Esteeming the Self and creativity

The great physicist Albert Einstein one day asked this
question: "Do you see the Universe as friendly or hostile?" This
was his way of distinguishing the optimists from the pessimists.
When we have done everything we can to accomplish a task or
complete a project but fail, the only thing we can do is trust in
the superabundance of the Universe. Rather than maintain a
defeatist attitude, those who esteem the Self entrust themselves
to a universal Intelligence.

A friend of mine who is director of a college was hiring
academic staff. She had hired six professors, but needed two
more. She had done everything she could think of, including advertising, and yet she could not fill these two positions.
Instead of getting uptight, she simply recognized her powerlessness, and asked Providence to provide. The next day she found
the two candidates she needed.

The creative intention is a spiritual strategy that consists
of exposing our need in a very concrete way to the Intelligence
of the Universe (which some people call God). Formulating a
detailed presentation of a need or a project will lead us to be on

The movement from self-esteem to esteeming the Self also means being more in communion with the Universe — that is, being more sensitive to conserving the universe in an ecological spirit.

the lookout for the occasions that favour its fulfillment. Once we have laid out our need or our project to the Universe, it is important that the ego stop fussing about it and detach itself from the request, as it is no longer the ego's responsibility.

The creative intention finds an echo in the way Jesus taught his disciples to pray, as recorded by Mark in his gospel: "So I tell you, whatever you ask for in prayer, believe that you have received it, and it will be yours" (Mark 11.24). A doctor confided to me that the recovery rate among his patients had increased since he had begun to spend a moment in meditation to ask for them to be healed; he pictured them being healed. By doing this he removed from himself any unconscious temptation to keep his patient dependent on him and to think of himself as the only one responsible for the patient's healing.

Esteeming the Self and "voluntary simplicity"

The movement from self-esteem to esteeming the Self also means being more in communion with the Universe — that is, being more sensitive to conserving the universe in an ecological spirit. Since the 1980s, a movement known as voluntary simplicity has existed. Its goal has been to promote ecology by combatting hyperconsuming, the draining of the planet's resources, and worldwide pollution. It invites people to become responsible for and respectful of the environment, and promotes the sharing of natural resources to benefit the whole of humanity, including future generations.

This movement takes its inspiration from a spirituality rooted in esteeming the Self. For more information, see the excellent work of Serge Mongeau, *La simplicité voluntaire, plus que jamais*.[41]

Esteeming the Self and adopting a spiritual vision of the world

*All problems lose their force
to the extent that you develop the habit of staying calm,
looking at and observing the divine harmony as it reveals itself.*

— JOEL S. GOLDSMITH

Esteeming the Self offers a broader perspective on difficult situations and problems.

Esteeming the Self offers a broader perspective on difficult situations and problems. It situates unhappy events in a wider context, to the point that they become less intense and sometimes even reveal a silver lining. This is called *spiritual reframing*. Instead of languishing in despair, people find they can discover a positive sense in any event, no matter how bad it might be. To tap into this potential, we must call on the Self and seek light and comfort in various thinkers and spiritual people that we trust.

Spiritual reframing is equally possible if approached from the angle of positive intention. I am always surprised by the results obtained through the method called *transformation at the heart of the self.* This method consists of calling on positive motivations hidden in faults, corruption or obsession. To identify them, I ask the client what intention they were pursuing through their destructive behaviour. Using a series of questions that enable us to focus more and more closely on the positive intention, we can unearth a primary spiritual motive that, because of unfortunate circumstances, has remained buried and fed the destructive behaviour.

Take the case of the alcoholic. I question him or her about the positive intention: "What do you get from drinking?" He or she responds, "It helps me relax." I follow that line of questioning on the positive intention: "What does relaxation do

We can discover the desire for the infinite and the sacred welling up from the depths of our being, from the Self.

for you?" The answer might be: "When I am really relaxed, I can finally be myself. I've always tried to please my father, even though his aspirations for me don't fit who I am."

In this way, we can discover the desire for the infinite and the sacred welling up from the depths of our being, from the Self. This desire for the Absolute that has remained camouflaged can be revealed in many different forms: a deep sense of inner unity, the feeling of being ourselves, the discovery of a unshake-able peace, the feeling of being accepted as we are, of being loved and of loving.[42]

CONCLUSION

Here, in summary, we will compare the attributes of the ego and the Self through the characteristics of a person driven by ego and one driven by the influence of the Self.

Ego	Self
Pursues goals with the help of willpower	Welcomes a spiritual awakening and peak experiences
Is motivated by survival and the fear of missing out on something	Opens the self to the bounty of creation
Uses intelligence and abilities in practical ways	Is radiant with love, wisdom, inner harmony and its own mission
Has a history made up of events that unfold in space and time	Expresses itself through symbols and universal, timeless myths
Is pulled apart by conflicting tendencies	Looks for peace and inner harmony
Sets its sights on competence, mastery of self and the environment	Hands itself over to a divine Intelligence
Tries to hang on to possessions	Strives for detachment from things
Counts on the efforts of will, daring and perseverance	Trusts in Providence
Makes progress thanks to its own efforts	Is open to the action of grace found in each moment
Wears a social mask, a persona, and compares itself to others	Is present to others and to the Universe
Seeks out competition	Looks for collaboration and solidarity
Experiences great anguish at the thought of death	Knows how to die and is convinced of rebirth

CHAPTER 12

The negative path for attaining the Self

We would be like sculptors preparing to sculpt.
They remove each obstacle to the pure vision of the hidden image,
and simply by this act of cleansing,
they reveal the hidden beauty.

— PSEUDO-DIONYSIUS

The negative path allows us to clear away useless attachments so that the action of the Self can take precedence. This is the goal of all self-emptying. The negative path is difficult to understand: however paradoxical it might appear, it does not lead to barrenness or death, but to fruitfulness and liberation of the power of the Self.

We need to become conscious of our experiences of loss, identify them, and mourn them.

How do we embark on this negative path? First, we need to become conscious of our experiences of loss, identify them, and mourn them. Doing so leads to esteeming the Self and liberating its energy. Instead of denying and repressing our losses, we are to welcome them.

By grieving these painful but transitory passages, we allow more intense life to emerge. If it is well understood and well managed, the emptiness and nothingness eventually lead to the fullness of the experience of the Self.

Other, more proactive, approaches in the negative way that we will examine include the process of disidentification, dear to the school of psychosynthesis, which strips the person of their superficial identity; the reintegration of the shadow, which involves sacrificing the ego; and deliberate detachments, sacrifices that allow us to pursue an ideal.

To live these losses well requires strong self-esteem.

LETTING GO

Music needs the holes of the flute;
letters need the white of the paper;
light needs the emptiness of windows.

— J. VERNETTE AND C. MONCELON

The spiritual way requires that we keep letting go

Our lives are strewn with losses. From birth to death, we live a series of losses: first, the inevitable losses as we grow up, and then unforeseen losses caused by illness, separations, accidents, and heartbreaks.

To live these losses well requires strong self-esteem. If we do not live these losses well, the grief that follows can lead to physical and psychological difficulties, even psychological illnesses and spiritual dead ends. People with low self-esteem live their losses neurotically. For example, they remain too attached — to people who have gone from their lives and to the past. Their lives seem to be on hold; they cling to the illusion that they can bring back their beloved ones; their psychological growth is stuck and their spiritual evolution stagnates.

People who love themselves and have self-confidence, meanwhile, are able to separate themselves from their loved ones, and from past situations. They do not forget these people, but construct a new and healthy relationship with them. The grieving process strips their ego from attachments that are too intense and establishes new spiritual links with those who have gone.

Why does the ego fear grief?

What the caterpillar calls the end of the world
the rest of the world calls a butterfly.

— RICHARD BACH

In grief, it is important to distinguish between the world of the ego and that of the Self. My book *How to Love Again: Moving from Grief to Growth*, outlines the stages of grief:

- first stage: shock
- second stage: denial
- third stage: expressing emotions and feelings
- fourth stage: completing the tasks related to grieving
- fifth stage: discovering the meaning of the loss
- sixth stage: forgiveness
- seventh stage: claiming the legacy
- eighth stage: celebrating the end of grief.[43]

Here I will simply identify which of these stages belong to the ego (to self-esteem), and which belong to the Self.

The task of the ego in coming to terms with grief consists in not allowing yourself to drown in the defence system put in place to survive the loss. The ego fears dying; it seeks to protect itself by triggering powerful defence mechanisms. Therapists who deal with death therefore speak of shock and of cognitive and affective denial. When the ego becomes more fully conscious of the loss and of its own powerlessness, it progressively abandons the blockage of its grief. When it becomes fully conscious of the loss, the ego plunges into expressing all sorts of emotions, such as sadness, powerlessness, anger, guilt, and distress. It lives in a state of depression and regression.

Grieving people who have strong self-esteem give themselves the right to live and to express all their emotions and feelings, not just certain ones; they count on their inner strength to allow themselves to regress temporarily and to live a period of depression. They are more conscious of the need to detach themselves from the person who was dear to them, or from a situation that was precious to them, but they know that they

Grieving people who have strong self-esteem give themselves the right to live and to express all their emotions and feelings, not just certain ones.

The role of the Self is to sustain us in the grieving process.

cannot overcome their grief without the help of the Self, which always accompanies them in distress.

The Self brings the hope of rebirth

Death does not destroy the ties woven during life.
It transforms them.

— JOHN MONBOURQUETTE

No one can let go of the people they love unless they hope to be reborn and to re-establish spiritual ties with them. Otherwise, they would be numb with grief in the face of the absence, the nothingness, the emptiness that is like a dark night. In this painful state, the role of the Self is to sustain us in the grieving process, for the Self knows that it is immortal, and that the state of mourning, however painful, is temporary. The Self always comforts the ego of those who mourn and who are in the throes of the process of detachment.

During therapy with grieving people, I have often been told of overwhelming situations. As they spoke of their grief, some felt invaded by images such as a black hole, a bleak desert, a devastated landscape, the bottom of a lake. I always encourage people to enter into these images and to identify with them. After a few moments of panic, their images are transformed into beams of light, green meadows, a beautiful landscape, a lake full of fish and aquatic plants. These transformations are the work of the Self, who gives new life to those who grieve.

Sometimes my grieving clients experience immense distress: they live the pain of dying with their beloved and even experience the same physical symptoms that led to the death. I accompany them through this symbolic death until they have lived it fully.

I attest with absolute certainty to the intervention of the Self, who comforts them, offers them peace and gives them the sense of coming back to life.

The Self, the person's deepest identity, cannot be fully grasped by the conscious self.

DISIDENTIFICATION

The spiritual journey consists of coming back to the beginning of ourselves, that is, to the experience of Being.

— RICHARD MOSS

We know that the Self, the person's deepest identity, cannot be fully grasped by the conscious self. Disidentification is a basic exercise in the school of psychosynthesis created by Roberto Assagioli. It consists of discovering what the Self is not, of intuiting our real identity by disengaging all that does not belong to our real identity, our Self. This process allows people to loosen their grip on and let go of all the false identities that they have been wearing, believing that these were an integral part of their being.

Often the misuse of the verb *to be* is responsible for these false identities. Many people mistakenly identify themselves with qualities, faults or roles that are not essential to their deepest identity. Thus, they may say, "I *am* generous," "I *am* shy," "I *am* hardworking," "I *am* an alcoholic" to mean that "I *have* the quality of generosity," "I *have* the characteristic of shyness," I *have* the virtue of working hard," "I *have* an addiction to alcohol." They imprison themselves in qualities, faults, social roles or professional functions that have nothing to do with their real identity.

Let us examine some of the positive effects of the exercise of disidentification. For example, if I have a migraine, it is important that I not identify myself with it, as if my whole

Disidentification, which is a form of meditation, helps us create a certain psychological distance from our problems and allows for greater self-mastery.

being has become a migraine. Therefore I will say, "I have a migraine, but I am not my migraine." Respecting this distinction allows for a better mastery of the pain. The same rule applies in the emotional world. When I am disappointed and I say to myself, "I have been disappointed, but I am not my disappointment, because I am more than my disappointment," I disidentify myself with it. I also avoid believing or letting others believe that my whole being is only sorrow or suffering. This exercise allows me to create a space of peace and freedom before physical or spiritual suffering.

Regularly practising disidentification will create a healthy detachment from the attributes that we believe we have, and that we have allowed others to convince us that we have. Disidentification, which is a form of meditation, helps us create a certain psychological distance from our problems and allows for greater self-mastery. Such practice leads to a stance of self-emptying that is comparable to that of Zen practioners.

REINTEGRATING THE SHADOW, OR THE SACRIFICE OF THE EGO

Manure is part of the flower.
It is a link in the chain of life that passes from darkness to light.
Manure allows the rose to reach its fullness.
The flower is manure that has been loved.

— PLACIDE GABOURY

The shadow comes to the aid of self-esteem

In the first part of this book, which dealt with self-esteem, self-confidence, and the affirmation of the self, we examined the possibility of the ego enjoying greater autonomy. Here we address the problem of an overly invasive persona interfering with the actions of the conscious self.

Thus, the ego's autonomy is dragged down by its preoccupation with dealing with the demands and expectations from the outside, especially those of parents, teachers, peers, and the surrounding culture. The ego experiences real or imagined fears of being rejected.

I do not want to imply here that high self-esteem depends only on strategies of self-esteem and self-confidence. However, these are the foundation of healthy, competent self-esteem. But to reinforce and strengthen self-esteem, and to progress towards esteeming the Self, it is important to reintegrate what has been repressed and to mine all its richness.

Reintegrating the shadow is essential to the development of solid self-esteem.

Reintegrating the shadow is essential to the development of solid self-esteem. The untamed forces of the shadow, which have been taken for granted, will always come back to consume the energy of the self and erode its esteem. To be able to harmonize the persona and the shadow, we must turn to the integrating energy of the Self, not to the willed efforts of the ego.

I am astounded that current books on self-esteem overlook the influence of the shadow. Left untamed, the shadow becomes a source of poor self-esteem and conflict with others.

Let us examine how the conscious self can reappropriate the qualities and resources that it has repressed. To know our shadow, to make peace with it and work with it constitutes one of the essential conditions of all healthy self-esteem and the beginning of esteeming the Self. We cannot truly love ourselves and have confidence in ourselves if we allow our shadow to sap our energy and act against our best interests.

The shadow is everything that we have repressed in our unconscious because we were afraid of being rejected by the key adults in our lives when we were young.

What is the shadow?

The shadow is the door to what is real.

— ELIE HUMBERT

The shadow is everything that we have repressed in our unconscious because we were afraid of being rejected by the key adults in our lives when we were young. We were afraid that certain aspects of our personality and behaviour would cause us to lose their affection, disappoint them or embarrass them. We soon learned what was acceptable and what was not acceptable in their eyes. To please them, we relegated large parts of ourselves to the forgotten corners of our unconscious. We did everything we could to avoid the least verbal or unspoken disapproval by those we loved and on whom we depended. We created a social mask for ourselves, a persona that seemed more acceptable to those around us.

The shadow develops according to the demands of our environment. It constitutes "the other in me," our buried alter ego, the unknown other self who lives in our unconscious. It is hidden, but not absent. It comes to light in unexpected ways, above all in dreams, in the form of bizarre and hostile symbols. It wants to be recognized, accepted, and reintegrated. If it remains misunderstood or ignored, it will manifest itself through anxiety attacks, inexplicable phobias, and projections onto others.

The shadow's garbage bag

The poet and thinker Robert Bly compares the personality's shadow to a garbage bag into which we throw aspects of ourselves that we consider unacceptable to people around us.[44] The so-called black shadow includes such instinctual expressions as sexuality and aggression, personality traits such as criminal attitudes, a tendency towards laziness, a propensity for disobedience. The "white" shadow takes in all our undeveloped moral and spiritual potential, such as qualities of patience, a work ethic, politeness; all kinds of talents and abilities; moral virtues; and, of course, spiritual longings.

If they do not work at reintegrating the shadow, people will fall prey to psychological illnesses.

The fear of rejection leads us to fill our garbage bag with all these things until we are in our thirties. In mid-life, when we are more mature and more self-assured, it is time to start emptying the garbage bag and recycle all the rich potential buried there.

The consequences of the untamed shadow

Carl Jung recalls the tragedies caused by the shadow that has lain fallow in the human psyche: "We know that the most moving and strangest dramas are not put on in the theatre but in the hearts of ordinary men and women. These go through life without attracting attention and betray none of the conflicts that are raging within them, unless they are overwhelmed by a depression that is always possible."[45]

If they do not work at reintegrating the shadow, people will fall prey to psychological illnesses. They will be tormented by a vague feeling of anxiety and dissatisfaction. They will feel stressed and depressed. They will allow themselves to be caught up in different drives: guilt, jealousy, poorly managed anger, resentment, inappropriate sexual behaviour, addictions, and so on. Among the most common addictions are to alcohol and drugs, two of the scourges of our society. In an excellent article on the causes of addiction, Sam Naifeh affirms that "Addiction is a problem of the shadow."[46] The compulsive attraction to alcohol and drugs gives access to the shadow side of our being. We may blame alcohol and drugs for human folly, but they are

Those who understand the necessity of reconciling themselves with their shadow will see the momentary fear that they experience transformed into joy when their self-esteem grows.

only indirect causes. They allow users to break through the barriers of the conscious self and make contact with their shadow.

Instead of handing ourselves over to the illusory paradises of drugs and alcohol (the word *alcohol* means *dream* in Arabic), we can do more effective and beneficial growth work by using some psychospiritual exercises that allow us to become conscious of our shadow and integrate it.

Recognizing the shadow and sacrificing the ego

Recognizing the shadow is the first step towards discovering the whole of our being. But confronting the shadow is no mean feat. Up to this point, all the ego's efforts have been deployed to assure its social and financial security, along with the control and domination of others. The ego fears being exposed as vulnerable and unstable, even unbalanced. It shudders at the thought of having to die to itself. Fear and anxiety are the price that the ego has to pay to accept facing its shadow and the misery it has been trying to mask. Those who have a false concept of self-esteem, who think it will protect them from all hardship, will perceive the shadow as a threat to the self.

Those, on the other hand, who understand the necessity of reconciling themselves with their shadow will see the momentary fear that they experience transformed into joy when their self-esteem grows.

The ego needs to accept that one day it will find itself caught between its persona, its social façade, and its shadow; between the demands of the outer and inner worlds. If it succeeds in having the two emerge and tolerating the inner tension that will follow, the Self will come to its rescue and offer it a kind of "resurrection." The intervention of the Self will take the form of an integrating symbol that will allow us to reconcile the demands of the persona with those of the shadow.

Such a reconciliation marks the beginning of *individuation*, the process by which we become "who we are," that is, become a unique personality, complete and independent from tyrannizing social influences. From the scattered and opposing elements of the psyche, the Self creates a new internal organization for us, or a new level of complexity of our being. Suddenly, we acquire greater maturity; we are more ourselves and better able to make use of our resources and resolve our conflicts. The Self gains for us peace and harmony that are beyond price.

From the scattered and opposing elements of the psyche, the Self creates a new internal organization for us.

Recognizing the shadow and its relationship with those whom we adore or detest

The theory of projection

The projection of the shadow is both a spiritual and a psychological phenomenon. As Marie-Louise von Franz says, "Jung defined projection as an unconscious transfer — that is, unperceived and involuntary — of repressed psychic elements onto an external object."[47] The projection consists of seeing, hearing, and feeling emotions, qualities, and traits that we have repressed in ourselves and reflecting them back onto an external object. This displaces repressed psychic material from the inside of the self to the outside of the self.

Psychoanalysis sees projection as a means of self-defence against the eventual spilling over of the shadow, above all in the form of anxiety. Everything that is unacceptable to the conscious will be found, sooner or later, outside the self, spread out and projected onto objects, animals or people. This explains the phobias that so many people have. The "projectors" — those doing the projection — are not conscious of what is happening and see the ghosts of their own psyche reflected on the object of their phobia.

Becoming conscious of what we project onto others is the key to accessing our elusive shadow.

The projectors, who are almost always unconscious of projecting onto the other, nevertheless perceive themselves as being gripped by something unhealthy. They are fascinated by a person, animal or object from which they are unable to detach their attention. They are either seduced or repulsed, depending on whether the characteristics of the other are considered to be desirable, troubling or threatening. Consequently, they will either idealize the other for their desirable qualities or detest them for the qualities they judge to be undesirable or repulsive. In both cases, seduction and repulsion, the projector's assessment will be distorted, because it will be disproportionate to the objective reality.

The projections of the shadow: a source of anxiety for the projector themselves

Becoming conscious of what we project onto others is the key to accessing our elusive shadow. Neglecting to recognize these projections blocks growth and social development. Every time we project elements of our shadow onto someone else, we alienate those elements from ourselves and consequently deprive ourselves of recognizing them as our own. Then we feel that we have lost part of ourselves.

At the same time that we adore or hate another person, we feel diminished. Whether positive or negative, these projections drain our energy; they can eventually cause burnout.

Those who have not mastered the art of reclaiming their projections close in on themselves. Those aspects of the shadow that they attribute to others come back on them, causing anxiety, depression, and conflicts in human relationships. These people's self-esteem and their interpersonal relationships take a battering.

Those who learn to reintegrate their projections into the conscious zone of their being will acquire invaluable knowledge of their shadow side as well as a new and greater harmony with their unconscious.

To my knowledge, no psychological test exists that is more revealing of the qualities and character traits that are missing in someone's personality than the examination of their projections. In other words, if we are driven to unduly despise or adore someone for certain qualities or character traits, it is a sign that we urgently need to develop these qualities in ourselves.

If we are driven to unduly despise or adore someone for certain qualities or character traits, it is a sign that we urgently need to develop these qualities in ourselves.

Let's take an example. If I hate someone who is gentle, calm, and unassuming, it is no doubt because these qualities, which would counterbalance the more aggressive aspects of my personality (such as my desire to be seen and my hectic life), are missing in me. Undoubtedly, at the beginning I will have to get over both my repugnance towards becoming gentle, calm, and modest, and the aversion I feel in having to become like someone I don't like. But once I have mastered the initial repulsion, I will be astonished to see everything that I can learn from this person that will bring me to greater maturity.

This process of reintegrating the shadow is not unlike homeopathy, the art of healing by ingesting a minimal amount of the poison that is at the root of the illness.

Recognizing the projections of the shadow is necessary for loving others

During a conference, Robert Bly noted the danger of projections. People who are the object of projections, he reminded his audience, can run a real danger for their reputation, moral integrity, and physical safety, and even for their life. In certain cases of fascination, they risk being adored to excess and developing illusions about themselves. On the other hand, those who

Even if the reintegration of the shadow seems painful for the ego, it is beneficial.

are the object of repulsion can become the scapegoat. This happens in families that need a black sheep to blame problems on so the others can survive. History witnesses to collective projections that have been the cause of atrocious crimes, cruel persecutions, and wars, such as the witch hunts that killed thousands of innocent women, or the Holocaust that killed six million people simply because they were Jews.

It is always possible to recover from projections

Can we be healed of the projections that we impose on others? Yes. The shadow is elusive, avoiding the subtlest consciousness, but we can become conscious of the fascination or repulsion that obsesses us. In doing so, we have a good chance of discovering the movements of the shadow and their meaning. Then it becomes possible to heal our projections: first, by recognizing their presence in us, and then by recovering them through appropriate exercises.

Spiritual poverty

Even if the reintegration of the shadow seems painful for the ego, it is beneficial. It allows for psychospiritual growth, notably in the area of spiritual poverty. Little by little, it breaks down the lovely façade created by the persona; it allows the character to be more flexible and softens the stiffness of perfectionism. In thus fostering spiritual poverty, the ego gradually recognizes its weaknesses and its moral vulnerability. It sees that it has the same instincts of envy, sexuality, and manipulation as other people do, and that it has the makings of the worst criminal or villain. Beyond its phariseeism, its pride, and its moral fanaticism, it becomes conscious that it has let itself be caught up in the desires of its shadow, and that it could easily have become the worst delinquent.

Recognizing our shadow allows us to come to a greater truth and simplicity about ourselves, and to be forevermore on guard against any pretensions to being perfect. Over time, we conquer the fear of revealing who we are. What is more, we learn not to blame others, and to judge them less severely. The acceptance of this shadowy, immature side allows us to develop greater humility and compassion towards others. We are less likely to throw stones at others. We recognize that the people around us are not nasty; rather, we see them as weak and wounded, like us, and recognize that they are living their lives to the best of their ability.

When we pursue our mission and an ideal with energy and enthusiasm, sacrifices are easy.

VOLUNTARY DETACHMENTS OR SACRIFICES

When the desire to take disappears,
jewels will appear.

— YOGA SUTRA

In the *via negativa*, or negative path, voluntary detachments are the equivalent of sacrifices that we embrace to attain a higher end.

This is the deep sense of the word *sacrifice*, according to its root, *sacrum facere*, "to make holy." The use of this word will undoubtedly cause a reaction in certain people. It may bring to mind useless renunciations imposed by the fantasies of parents and teachers, designed to impose a sullen form of masochism or offer a sacrifice to a capricious divinity. But the expression "make a sacrifice" has always had another meaning: to renounce certain benefits for the sake of a higher goal, particularly those goals that belong to the Self.

When we pursue our mission and an ideal with energy and enthusiasm, sacrifices are easy. In the drive to realize our soul's

Voluntary sacrifices are in tune with the intentions of the Self, which is constantly in relationship with the Universe.

dream, they are almost imperceptible. They become hard to deal with when we are unsure of our mission or our ideal, or when we despair of achieving our goal.

The sacrifices we must make depend on our circumstances. Perhaps we have to postpone immediate gratification, accept a lower salary, cut spending, allow our tranquility to be disturbed, set aside our independence to work as part of a team, agree to live far away from friends and family, give up pleasures and leisure activities, put aside preconceived ideas and prejudices, know how to be patient and to live with insecurity.

Earlier I spoke about the choice of voluntary simplicity for the sake of the ecology. This simplicity of life combats hyper-consumption and is content with a modest lifestyle. These voluntary sacrifices are in tune with the intentions of the Self, which is constantly in relationship with the Universe.

CONCLUSION

To love oneself humbly . . .
It is part of the human condition to be wounded and powerless.
Are we guilty of being a man or a woman?
The first response to our limitations
should not be blame,
but very gentle, very humble, very serene acceptance.

— JACQUES LECLERC

The promises made to those who commit themselves to the *via negativa*, the negative path, are many. We have seen that our grief leads us to become conscious of our vulnerability, to the point that we may become depressed or experience distress. But the Self knows how to achieve rebirth when, at last, we let go.

Disidentification teaches us to unmake our false identity. It is a difficult task to stop identifying ourselves with our emotions, our malaise, our psychological difficulties, our reputation or our social standing, however honourable these may be, by the strength of our thoughts, the certainty of our loves, and so on. The distance that we put between ourselves and these passing inner and outer realities allows us to appreciate the stability of the Self.

As the Self intervenes, the path of detachment leads to unexpected openings and moments of grace and creativity.

The identification of our shadow, the wounded side of our being, allows us to become conscious of our inner poverty, which keeps us humble. When we sacrifice the ambitions of our ego so that we can face both our greatest misery and our noblest aspirations, we take one more step towards the Self.

The daily and deliberate acceptance of the sacrifices that enable us to fulfill our mission or our ideal delay many gratifications of the ego. We thus become accustomed to a life of patience and simplicity.

Self-satisfaction, smug contentment, the lack of risk-taking, and the anxious search for perfection create in us closed hearts and spirits.

As the Self intervenes, the path of detachment leads to unexpected openings and moments of grace and creativity.

Charles Péguy wrote this about "honest people … or those who describe themselves in that way": "They hardly show the openness inflicted by a terrible wound, unforgettable distress, a mistake that can't be corrected, a stitch that will never heal cleanly, a fatal worry, an unshakeable lurking anxiety, a secret bitterness, a breakdown that has been covered up, an unhealed scar." He concludes, "They do not offer an opening for grace."

CHAPTER 13

The positive, symbolic path to the Self

The fulfillment of the Self depends on whether we welcome attentively its subtle promptings and directions. Coming to know the Self, its deep identity, is not the result of logic, rationality or the will, but of an intelligent sensitivy that can grasp its messages and their symbolic meaning. This process should not surprise us, since it follows the typical functioning of the Self.

There are effective means of progressing on the positive path.

Some of the manifestations of the Self include spiritual insights, dreams and daydreams, sudden awakenings of the soul through reading spiritual stories and myths, projection on and attachment to symbolic figures, fantasies, fleeting experiences of a new Presence, marvelling at nature, a progressive awakening of our own spiritual life and that of others, an intense joy at being alive, a feeling of being loved unconditionally, contemplating the mystery of ordinary things, new delight in the real, and insights into the divine. Paying attention to the Self and to its symbolic signs is not an easy skill to develop, as these signs often go unnoticed by those who are not attuned to them.

As in the negative path, there are effective means of progressing on the positive path. We will look at the following approaches closely: using active imagination for working with symbols, studying our dreams, reconciling contradictory symbols, making mandalas, and becoming familiar with universal myths and the stories of the mystics.

THE ACTIVE IMAGINATION

Carl Jung recommends that those who want to develop their consciousness set up a dialogue between their conscious and unconscious by means of active imagination. This method allows them to take into account messages from the unconscious (dreams, fantasies, projections, etc.) and to translate them into

The active imagination bridges the conscious and the unconscious and unveils a secret to the unconscious.

some kind of artistic medium, such as discussion, drawing, painting or sculpture. Using active imagination, consciousness looks closely at the symbolic messages that flow from the unconscious, particularly those that come from the shadow, from the *anima/animus* and, ultimately, from the Self.

Initially, the person chooses a symbolic message from a dream or daydream. Then, they contemplate it, even if they do not understand it. The simple fact of concentrating on the symbol transforms it. For example, if someone focuses attention on the symbolic image of a snake that appeared in a dream, they will note that the snake changes colour, comes alive, tries to trigger a reaction and express itself. Active imagination sets off a psychological process that reveals the unconscious. Thus, it is important to constantly note the changes taking place in the symbolic image of the snake. This image in motion reveals what is happening in the unconscious. With the aid of active imagination, the person remains in the sphere of the conscious mind, even as they watch an unconscious process unfolding before their eyes. The active imagination bridges the conscious and the unconscious and unveils a secret to the unconscious.

Let us examine the process of active imagination. After contemplating the symbol, the subject enters into relationship with the symbolic reality, and asks what it means. Let's continue with our example of the snake. The dreamer enters into a dialogue with the snake and asks it to identify itself. He asks what the snake wants of him. Thus dialogue and collaboration between the dreamer and the symbol of the snake are established, bearing a message from the unconscious.

If the dreamer defines himself as someone who is very gentle, the snake will remind him that there exists within him an unconscious aggression that drains his energy and causes him anxiety that will make him depressed. The snake concedes that unconscious suffering is possible, and eventually reveals the existence of a tragedy in the dreamer's life. With this better knowledge of the two sides of himself, the dreamer is better able to keep his life in balance, make more enlightened decisions, maintain more authentic human relationships and discover meaning in life.

Dreams let us see a different point of view about ourselves, one that we don't want to see.

Why bother going through the work of the active imagination? The symbolic figure reveals a hidden side of the self; it tends to help us see what we hide, the repressed part of the self. It allows us to discover the whole of our conscious and unconscious reality, and thus completes the partial, truncated vision of the conscious.

STUDYING DREAMS

Through dreams, the Self corrects and complements the perception of the biased view of the ego. Dreams let us see a different point of view about ourselves, one that we don't want to see. That is why it is often painful to understand our dreams, listen to them, and unearth their meaning.

It is best not to try to interpret dreams rationally, for rational interpretations often misread the symbolic messages of dreams. For this reason, it is enough to remember our dreams and to write them down when we wake up. Such simple gestures indicate to the unconscious and, ultimately, to the Self, that we are taking their messages seriously even if we don't yet grasp their full meaning.

While I was writing this book, I was involved in a number of other things as well. One night I dreamt that I had to transport people in a tiny car that was already full of luggage and of plates containing hot food. When I awoke, I experienced a

The Self possesses great integrating force. It can free the psyche that is stuck between two realities that appear to be opposing.

deep sense of being weighed down in my life. That morning I cancelled two projects in which I was involved.

If remembering dreams and recording them in a journal isn't enough, people can recount their dreams to themselves while identifying with each part of the dream. For the dream I just described, the narration would go like this: "I am carrying people who are all me, in a little car that is me, full of luggage and hot plates that are also me." Listing characters and objects in a dream reveals potential psychological conflicts.

Another method consists of choosing a symbolic figure that is central to my dream — for instance, the little car — and dialoguing with it using the method of active imagination described above.

RECONCILIATION OF OPPOSITES USING AN INTEGRATING SYMBOL

How can human beings
integrate the interior life into their development?
Either by reconciling emotional or intellectual conflicts
into a higher synthesis
or by reconciling diversity
into a more complete unity.

— ALDOUS HUXLEY

The Self possesses great integrating force. It can free the psyche that is stuck between two realities that appear to be opposing: joy and sorrow, love and hate, fear and a taste for adventure, feelings of repulsion and attraction, sexual desire and chastity, wanting to live and wanting to die. Many people are paralyzed by the tug of war between these opposing forces because they do not know how to get themselves out of it.

Some try to resolve the issue by reasoning, but in vain, because the task is bigger than reason. Only by turning to the Self can they resolve the dilemma. All they have to do is ask the Self to produce for them a numinous (religious) integrating symbol.

Only by turning to the Self can they resolve the dilemma.

Using a test developed by Mario Berta, entitled *symbolic perspective in psychotherapy*, I developed a strategy that can integrate the persona and the shadow. This exercise illustrates well the importance of turning to symbols to reconcile opposing realities.

a) To begin, I ask participants to relax and centre on themselves.

b) After recommending that they allow a response to emerge spontaneously from their imagination, I ask this question: "If you were in another world and could choose another identity, what symbolic being would you like to become?" This symbolic being could be a thing, a plant, an animal, or some kind of fictional character, but not a real person.

c) After they have had a few minutes of concentration, I ask those who have found the symbol that expresses their new identity to raise their hands. If necessary, I give the group more time. Then I ask participants to come out of their centred experience.

d) Each person finds a partner to whom they describe their symbol for a few minutes. The listener is authorized to ask factual questions about their partner's symbol: How big is it? What colour? Does it move? Make noise? Come close or stay far way? What background is it set against? In what context? Once the first person has finished describing their symbol, their partner describes their own symbol.

e) I then invite participants to centre themselves again, and to answer the following question: "If you were in another world and if you could choose another identity, what being would

I invite them to ask for the collaboration of the Self to help them integrate their positive and negative symbols without thinking or reasoning.

you hate to become? It can be a thing, a plant, an animal, or fictional character, but not a real person. You would not want to become such a being because you are very afraid, or you find it thoroughly repulsive."

f) Once they have found the negative symbol, they move out from their centred state, and share their symbol with their partner.

g) After this exchange, I ask each participant to find a quiet place in the room.

h) Then I invite them to raise their hands in front of their chest and hold them about thirty centimeters from each other. For a minute or two, they look at their right hand, where they imagine they are holding their positive symbol. Then they look at their left hand, where they imagine they are holding their negative symbol.

i) Next I invite them to ask for the collaboration of the Self to help them integrate their positive and negative symbols without thinking or reasoning.

j) I ask them to let their hands come closer together spontaneously and naturally. I encourage them to let themselves be surprised by the sudden appearance of a third symbol that the Self will form following the integration of the two others.

If some people feel that their hands resist coming together, I advise them to find out what is between their hands that might be causing this resistance and eliminate it before they continue with the exercise.

k) When everyone has completed the integration of their positive and negative symbols, I invite them to share their discoveries with the group or with their partner. Some people like to draw their symbol as a reminder of the integration that has taken place.

A word of caution to any readers who are counsellors or facilitators. If a participant does not succeed in doing this exercise of reintegration, do not force them to do it. It may be that the unconscious is not ready to reintegrate the shadow, or that the negative symbol is too strong and therefore paralyzing. In the latter situation, it would be appropriate to find a way to reduce the impact of the negative symbol, by modifying its proportions, for example. One counsellor did this with a woman who felt powerless to integrate her positive symbol with her negative one, an immense boa. He invited her to imagine that the size of the boa had been reduced to acceptable dimensions. After doing so, the client successfully completed the exercise.

The mandala is a symbolic figure representing a circle that has a centre, around which are arranged a group of shapes.

I am always astonished by the results of this exercise. Most participants usually succeed in obtaining from the Self an integrating sacred symbol that appears to resolve the tension between the positive and negative symbols: a luminous cup, a temple full of light, a winged dragon, a child's shining face, or another theme found in the myths whose stories are well known. This peak experience pulls them out of a psychic swamp, gives meaning to their life, and pushes them towards a personal mission.

THE MANDALA, A SYMBOL OF THE SELF

The mandala is a symbolic figure representing a circle that has a centre, around which are arranged a group of shapes. This figure is found everywhere in the universe, from plant cells to the rose windows of cathedrals to the nebulae of the stars. The mandala expresses at the same time unity and diversity.

*Carl Jung saw
in the symbol of
the mandala a
confirmation of his
theory of the Self.*

Carl Jung saw in the symbol of the mandala a confirmation of his theory of the Self:

> [...] by the very fact of sensing the existence of a centre of the personality, a sort of focal point in the psyche to which everything makes reference, by which everything is organized and which is in itself a source of energy. This central energy is shown by a compulsion, a quasi-irresistible impulse to become who we are, just as each organism is pushed to assume the characteristic form of its species, regardless of the circumstances.[48]

Jung continues, describing the form of the psyche's development. "There is scarcely any linear evolution, but only a circular approach, *walking in a circle* which gives, by its constant reference to this centre called the Self, structure, orientation and meaning."[49]

The mandala has often been compared to an eye that looks at the interior of the psyche. Because of its unifying response in the person, several religions have made it a sacred symbol. It adequately represents the complexity of the psyche: the centre that signifies the Self organizes the different parts of the psyche.

The practice of meditating on mandalas and of drawing them contributes to unifying the person, giving rise to the need to organize around the Self the scattered aspects of the psyche. The whole person thus feels himself or herself getting well and recovering his or her inner unity. This puts an end to the inner tensions caused by the fragmentations or splits in the personality.[50]

The mandala has often been compared to an eye that looks at the interior of the psyche.

THE EXPERIENCE OF MYTHS AND SPIRITUAL STORIES

Along with the above methods that draw on the richness of symbols — active imagination, dream work, discovering an integrating symbol and the mandala — an additional secular method cares for and nourishes the soul: knowledge of the great myths (the Greek word *mythos* means *story*) and religious stories.

In every age the mystics of the great religions have used stories to hand on indescribable religious experiences. These include Hasidic tales, gospel parables, Sufi short stories, and Buddhist stories.

In *The Search for the Beloved,* Jean Houston describes the beneficial effects of the classic spiritual stories of humanity. "The

The great stories of humanity enrich our life with relationships, models, and metaphors that allow us to understand our existence and give it meaning.

great stories of humanity are like energy fields charging the different events of our personal lives with meaning and significance. ... These great stories play on our spirits like a symphony, voicing different tones, themes, feeling and fantasies, and illuminating parts of ourselves that have been forgotten."[51]

If our own personal story seems insignificant and uninteresting, the great stories bring us a new inspiration that renews the pattern of our lives and gives them universal stature. The great stories of humanity enrich our life with relationships, models, and metaphors that allow us to understand our existence and give it meaning. They allow us to pass from our individual world, enclosed in a limited life, to a universal yet personal, human existence. Inspired by the myths and stories of humanity, we identify with Prometheus, Percival, Oedipus, Antigone, Ulysses, Isis, Rumi, Jesus, Buddha, Faust, and others.

Although Jean Houston uses strategies for growth that are psychological, she emphasizes in her workshops that using myths and stories speeds up the spiritual growth of her clients. These stories act on different levels of our being and contain messages and models of functioning that belong to the Self. Houston doesn't stop at reading the great myths; she has participants in her workshops act them out. She calls this type of intervention *Therapeia.* It belongs to her school of psychology, which she calls Sacred Psychology.

Guided imagery is another invaluable tool for moving from the ego to the Self. Ralph Metzner lists eleven mythical themes that can be used as images. Here is a summary of them:

1. From caterpillar to butterfly
2. From sleep and dreams to an awakening to reality
3. From the veil of illusion to the rediscovery of the real
4. From captivity to freedom

5. From pollution to purification by fire
6. From darkness to light
7. From fragmentation to unity
8. From aimlessness to a place of empowerment and vision
9. From alienation to a sense of being at home
10. From death to rebirth
11. From seed to tree of life.[52]

Symbolic language gives us an inner experience and has a tendency to stimulate the unconscious and, as a result, to liberate the action of the Self.

CONCLUSION

One day, a student asked Jean Houston, my teacher in transformational psychology, "Why do we have to talk to the Self using symbolic language and not intellectual concepts? We don't have control of the relationship when we speak in symbols, stories and myths." Jean replied, "Rational language is only understood by the intellect; in any case, if we spoke the language of the ego, the transformation of the person would not happen. Many people know what to do to grow spiritually; they have learned this through books and lectures but they still can't manage to do it." Symbolic language, as described above, gives us an inner experience and has a tendency to stimulate the unconscious and, as a result, to liberate the action of the Self. We may have self-control but not Self control; it is the Self that determines our spiritual growth.

CHAPTER 14

The influence of the Self: Unconditional love, wisdom, mission, and healing

An emir decided to leave his desert land to visit California. The travel agent strongly suggested that he visit Yosemite National Park. Accompanied by his chauffeur and his bodyguard, he set out for this region of primitive beauty.

At the park, he admired Bridalveil Falls. He marvelled at its elegance, its height, and the many rainbows that lived in its mist. He spent several hours contemplating this natural wonder. His chauffeur sent his chief bodyguard to tell him that it was getting late and they should be returning to the hotel. The emir exclaimed, "But the water hasn't stopped falling yet!"

— AUTHOR UNKNOWN

Archetypes are complexes that we live, that appear like a destiny in our personal life.

— CARL JUNG

Jung's discovery of the collective unconscious was one of the causes of disagreement between him and Freud. Freud, who believed that what was important was the personal unconscious formed principally by the repression of the Oedipal complex, declared Jung a heretic. Freud explained the origin of all artistic and religious works by sublimation, in which he saw a defensive reaction against the energies of the libido. Thanks to the study of dreams, myths, religion, alchemy, and various philosophies, particularly Chinese and Hindu, Jung opposed Freud's rather simplistic position. Jung had concluded that there existed an immense unconscious reservoir made up of images and symbols common to all humanity — that is, of a collective unconscious inhabited by symbolic themes that are present, with

Jung concluded that there existed an immense unconscious reservoir made up of images and symbols common to all humanity.

165

The Self has been described as "the royal archetype," "the image of the divine" in the soul.

some variations, in all human beings. He called these themes *archetypes*, or *primordial images* and *fundamental ideas*. These archetypes resemble Plato's inborn ideas. The French philosopher Henri Bergson called them *the eternal uncreateds*.

Jung made a distinction between archetypes per se and archetypes that are actualized by symbols. The former cannot be perceived, although they are potentially present in the structures of the psyche. They are invariable cores of meaning. The latter can be perceived through symbols, representations, and mythic themes.

Let us take the example of the archetypal theme of *father*. In itself, the archetype is an invisible energy form within both men and women, the organizational centre of all their latent paternal aspects. But the archetype of the father is actualized and takes shape within the person when she or he experiences paternal behaviour. They recognize paternal gestures instinctively and can get an idea of what a father is from them. This is how the archetypal image of the father is formed in a person.

Archetypes can be established in either positive or negative forms. If our experiences of paternal behaviours are positive, we will have the archetypal idea of a "good father"; if, on the other hand, they are negative, we will instead have the archetypal idea of a bad father or an ogre who devours his offspring.

The Self has been described as "the royal archetype," "the image of the divine" in the soul. Ideally, the Self is at the centre of the organization of the archetypes and co-ordinates its actions. It has no direct influence on the person, but is actualized and acts by means of archetypes. Let us illustrate this concept by describing four archetypes that serve the Self: the archetype of the "good Father" and "good Mother," who both assure unconditional love of the self; the "Wisdom figure," who gives meaning to all of life; the "inner Guide," who helps us discover our personal mission; and "the inner Healer," who resolves all the psychic conflicts that lead to sickness.

UNCONDITIONAL LOVE OF SELF AND OF OTHERS: TO LOVE AND BE LOVED

Let us weep for the world's oldest dream,
Let it laugh, let it make us shiver,
Let us burn our fingers on it,
Let us dance it and take it on our knees,
The oldest dream: to be loved.
Without reason. Without merit. Like that.

— CHRISTIANE SINGER

This question constantly comes up with people in therapy: "Am I lovable? Am I loved?"

Self-love depends on the belief that we feel lovable and loved unconditionally. This is the paramount religious feeling. Viktor Frankl affirms that the feeling of being loved in a totally unearned way is a peak experience.

It is love of the Self that unceasingly gives the sense of being lovable and loved. The Self is the womb in which the ego flourishes. It is the Self that becomes our best friend, who surrounds us with attention, encourages us, and proves to be a nourishing parent. In short, it takes charge of our insecure ego. The Self is our secret loving authority in the service of our ego.

Some "spiritual" people distort this image when they speak of putting the ego to death for the sake of the Self. This violent language frightens the ego, making it fearful before the

Self-love depends on the belief that we feel lovable and loved unconditionally.

167

If children receive signs of love and appreciation, they will learn to receive and integrate them.

Self. We cannot love ourselves unless we are conscious of being loved by the Self.

Certain people might say, "Why, then, do so many people not love themselves, and even worse, hate themselves?" Because to be activated, love of Self needs mediation and human intermediaries. The archetype of the Self is an unconscious energy that waits for experiences of unconditional love from the adults in their lives. If parents and other key adults raise a child in a climate of non-love, the love of Self, although always present, remains inhibited and inoperative. The child will develop a tyrannical superego that will keep him or her acting out of obligation and lead to discouragement and despair. The classic example is that of the delinquent who is discouraged because he has never been able to satisfy a despotic, loveless, oppressive superego. Ultimately, he will have no other choice but to rebel against authority.

Mediations to help people see themselves as loved and lovable are key to this purpose. If children receive signs of love and appreciation, they will learn to receive and integrate them. Thanks to such experiences of unconditional love, children will construct within themselves an inner parent or the archetype of an affectionate, kind parent. Then the Self assumes the form of the "good father" or "good mother," or both at once, an inexhaustible source of self-love.

We can evaluate the success of formation or therapy by the degree of tenderness and love that the subject experiences. This person will have learned to self-parent through the loving influence of the intervener. This is what happened to a young woman who had endured the pressure of her parents' ambition, but had never experienced their love. She had built up such a tyrannical and critical superego that she believed she was evil, and wanted to commit suicide. The unconditional love of her counsellor and of a friend taught her to love herself and free herself from suicidal thoughts. She succeeded in getting in touch with her Self. In her Self she could see a nurturing inner parent. Afterwards, whenever she felt overwhelmed by criticism, she would take refuge with this inner parent. Here she would feel completely accepted despite her vulnerabilities, faults, and unattractiveness. John Firman goes so far as to use the word *person* to describe the Self: "This is a person who loves us, guides us and, perhaps most importantly, respects our free will."[53]

When we allow the Self to exercise its loving influence, it evokes a radical feeling of self-love.

A woman in her forties confided to me that during a session of therapy she had the physical experience of being loved. Until that moment, she had believed that she was lovable because she of her willingness to help others, especially her suicidal mother. She finally understood deep within herself that she was worthy of unconditional love and started to self-parent. She told me, "I have always been a generous person, but my way of being has changed. I was someone who put myself last and was compulsively generous. As a result, I was always drained by the burdens of others. Now I am generous towards myself first, and towards others in a deliberate way."

When we allow the Self to exercise its loving influence, it evokes a radical feeling of self-love. In his book *Forget and Forgive*, Lewis Smedes shows that this fundamental feeling is something unique that does not resemble any other form of self-love. It is a radical love, because it establishes, more than any other experience, the feeling of being known and esteemed for what is deepest in us. We feel loved for no reason, despite our ugliness, our faults, our failures, and our transgressions. We know that we are bound to and inseparable from the Source of Love. This love, which is stronger than pleasure, joy and self-

Self-love, whose source always remains the love of the Self, reaches dimensions that are almost beyond imagining.

satisfaction, points to the warm feeling of security and trust in existence itself. Although we feel some moments of legitimate guilt for our faults or mistakes, the feeling of being accepted and forgiven once and for all overrides everything else. It offers us the assurance that we will never lose this source of infinite love. We always know that we can drink from this source and feel confirmed in love.

Self-love, whose source always remains the love of the Self, reaches dimensions that are almost beyond imagining. If self-esteem enables the love of others, the love of the Self increases ten-fold the intensity of love of others. Once we have discovered the love of the Self, we will be in a position to live the love that forgives.

The process of forgiving, which demands an outpouring of love, is both a human enterprise and a divine gift. Just as with grief, the participation of both the ego and the Self is required in forgiveness: the ego, so it can be healed of its wound; and the Self, so that we can love with superhuman generosity.

THE TWO GREAT MOMENTS OF FORGIVENESS

Healing our self-esteem

First, make peace with yourself,
so that you may then bring peace to others.

— THOMAS À KEMPIS

As Margaret Holmgren points out,[54] it is essential that the healing of self-esteem under the guise of self-respect begin with forgiveness. If not, forgiveness is illusory and unattainable.

It is important to recognize that self-esteem and self-respect have been damaged by the offender. Some people, under the pretext of forgiveness, deny that they have been hurt and repress the hurt in various ways: they make excuses for the offender; they feel guilty for provoking him; they try to forget; they want to appear magnanimous. Because they do not want to contemplate the humiliation and shame to their self-esteem and dignity, they betray themselves anew by refusing to admit their wounded feelings.

In my book *How to Forgive*, I describe in detail the psychological tasks that contribute to healing an offence. I will emphasize here a key step: forgiving ourselves. One of the disastrous consequences of an offence is identifying the self with the offender. Oddly enough, the victim is "contaminated" by the offensive acts to that point the he or she wants to do these same acts to others, particularly the offender, as a form of vengeance or self-punishment. In this context, forgiving oneself means reconciling within oneself the offender and the victim: stopping the offender in oneself and breaking free of victimization.

In other words, before they can even think of forgiving the offender, people who are hurt must re-establish their own harmony, which has been shattered by the offence. To do this, the offended person needs to call on a higher authority than that of the ego, which is caught at the same time in the role of offender and victim. It is the Self that can extricate the ego from this impasse and recreate its unity in order to prepare it to finally experience the divine gift of knowing that one is forgiven.

Before they can even think of forgiving the offender, people who are hurt must re-establish their own harmony, which has been shattered by the offence.

Experiencing unconditional love

Today people are asking, Is forgiveness possible without God's help? Some humanistic psychologists say yes, reducing forgiveness to a simple therapeutic technique. In my opinion, this position is dangerous. It diverts forgiveness from its true purpose: rising above the offender through love. This profound

The forgiver delights in the grace of the Self, who bestows a particular kind of love that is superior to all human love.

feeling of being unconditionally loved and forgiven by the Self allows people to make such a generous gesture. The sacred authority of the Self, nurtured by all the experiences of forgiveness throughout life, makes such a sublime gesture possible. After all, how can we love if we do not know the feeling of having been loved freely? How can we forgive if we do not have the deep conviction of having been unconditionally forgiven ourselves?

The forgiver delights in the grace of the Self, who bestows a particular kind of love that is superior to all human love. Receiving this love enables the forgiver to forgive in turn. This human form of forgiveness is but the echo of the forgiveness of the Self, the image of God within. In a sense, the forgiver is not the source of the forgiveness being extended, but a vessel that allows the divine pardon to pass through him or her.

ACQUIRING WISDOM

What is the meaning of my life? What are my reasons for living? Carl Jung argued that more than a third of his clients were looking for meaning for their lives. He affirmed that their many neuroses originated in the emptiness they were feeling. In his words, "A neurosis should be understood as a suffering of the soul that has not discovered its reason for being."[55]

Later, Victor Frankl put forth a similar argument. He asked his clients rather directly, "What stops you from committing suicide?" He thus forced them to express their reasons for living. Frankl reported the conclusions of a study whose outcome indicated that more than 55 per cent of patients suffered from one form or another of existential emptiness. He described these ailments of the soul in terms of an *existential vacuum* or *existential frustration,* and he called them *noogenic neuroses* (*nöos* refers to the spirit).

By referring to the archetype of the sage we can respond to the question of the meaning of life. Some people find answers in the great traditional religions or in philosophical propositions. But for how long? Loss of faith and of trust in life will aggravate their existential distress.

People react to the inner emptiness in different ways. They are at the mercy of the merchants of happiness. Some distract themselves by overconsuming, gambling, using drugs or pursuing sexual adventures. Others put themselves to sleep with distractions in Pascal's sense of the term. Some look for life's meaning in sects and their gurus. Others declare that life is absurd and contemplate suicide. Frankl's antidote to this vacuum of the soul is the "will to meaning." Frankl came to this wisdom in the Nazi concentration camps of World War II, where he recognized that when prisoners lost a reason for living, they let themselves die or committed suicide. The will to meaning, far from being an abstract idea or theory, is an ongoing passion for living.

Logotherapy, the school established by Frankl, teaches that to give meaning to life, people must learn to (i) discover their mission, their contribution to the community; (ii) experience the values of love, creativity, communion with nature; and (iii) find a reason for being in suffering. Self-actualization does not seem to Frankl to be a profitable path towards finding a reason to live. He sees in it the danger of being turned in on the self and going around in circles.[56] From my perspective, I do not view self-actualization as a threat if it ends in transcendence, on the Wholly-Other. Jung, for example, spent his whole life searching for himself. His reflection ended in the discovery of

We should not fall into the utopia of pretending that it is always easy to find meaning in life.

the transcendent Self. This is the route he describes in *Modern Man in Search of a Soul*, which he wrote in his prime.

The meaning of suffering

We should not fall into the utopia of pretending that it is always easy to find meaning in life. At certain moments, life appears meaningless, such as during periods of great unhappiness, or when we have experienced a major loss or have been deeply wounded. We feel lost. It is important to find an ear that will listen as we pour out our emotions. After we have been strengthened by this affective support, and only after, our listener can call on the wisdom of our Self. They will do this by asking the following questions, inviting us to allow responses to well up from the wisdom of the Self:

- Have you learned something about suffering from the loss or the hurt that you experienced?
- What new resources for life have you discovered within yourself?
- What limitations or fragility have you discovered in yourself? How have you succeeded in dealing with them?
- Have you become more human and compassionate towards others?
- What new degree of maturity have you attained?
- Into what has this ordeal initiated you?
- What new reasons for living has it given you?
- How much has this wound revealed to you the depth of your soul?
- From now on, how will you live your life?

I am always astonished at the original and constructive reflections, full of meaning for life, that my clients give in response to these questions.

DISCOVERING OUR MISSION

Try, with God's help,
to perceive the connection — even physical and natural —
that links your work to the building of the kingdom of heaven.

— TEILHARD DE CHARDIN

The abandonment of the ego to the Self allows us to discover our life project in our heart's persistent inclinations towards a certain activity in service of others.

Mission — also called *vocation* and *vision* — requires an inner guide, another archetype of the Self, in order to be realized. The abandonment of the ego to the Self allows us to discover our life project in our heart's persistent inclinations towards a certain activity in service of others. This inner guide, in addition to maintaining this inclination, puts us in contact with the Universe and makes us sensitive to the needs of those around us. It encourages us to develop our energies and talents for the good of the community.

The distinctive characteristics of mission

Identity: the origin of mission

Your vision will become clear
only if you see into your heart.
Whoever looks outward loses themselves in dreams;
whoever looks within awakens.

— CARL JUNG

John Firman writes: "The Self intentionally gives me [...] my individuality and my freedom, my conscience and my will — it gives me 'myself.' The Self does not try to imprison me or to snuff me out, but allows me to realize my unique character, my freedom and my vocation in life."[57] This text reveals the link between mission and identity. The Self gives identity, and the

The passion that characterizes mission has something of the permanent about it.

archetype of the inner guide gives the intuition for our mission.

Some people tend to equate mission with notoriety or stardom. For them, social success and popularity are signs of the authenticity of their mission. But mission cannot be identified with a social persona. Mission is born of the intuitions of the Self and is directed to the service of others. Undoubtedly mission needs to be recognized by the community, but it must not be confused with notoriety.

Mission is revealed by persistent passion

Personal mission takes on diverse forms: a passion, an ideal to pursue, an important goal to attain, a profound and persistent desire, a lasting inclination of the soul, an overflowing enthusiasm for a certain activity. The passion that characterizes mission has something of the permanent about it. Far from being a passing fancy or a pathological deviance, it becomes the soul-dream that pursues us, even when we refuse it. It is like a destiny that we can, unfortunately, deny and refuse.

The awareness of our mission is a peak experience

When the awareness of or the intuition about our mission strikes, we are caught up in a wave of enthusiasm, a surge of energy characteristic of a peak experience.

This breakthrough of the Self can arouse in the ego the anguish of having to abandon itself. In the midst of this enthusiasm, the ego fears the adventure of the mission; it panics when faced with the unknown and is afraid of losing the security it has acquired. The Muslim Indian sage Kabir wrote: "What God murmurs to the flower, he must shout into the ears of humans...." This mixture of enthusiasm and fear is an indicator of the sacred character of the reality to be lived.

The mission puts us in contact with the Universe

One man who had just come to terms with his mission was so moved that he began to weep. He said, "I have found my place in the world. I'll never have to compare myself with others and be jealous of them again."

The discovery and pursuit of our mission gives us a reason to live, brings meaning to life, and builds self-esteem and self-confidence. We then become conscious that our life-project has more far-reaching effects than we would have thought. In realizing our mission, we find ourselves connected with energy fields that are linked to the Universe.

By saying yes to the call of our inner guide, we enter into the movement of co-creation of the Universe. We participate in that universal intelligence and wisdom called Providence.

THE FUNCTION OF HEALING

The Self also has the function of healing the person and others thanks to the archetype of the "inner healer." In biomedicine, the caregiver's ideal is the physical *cure* of the illness or of the sick organ. The spiritualist-doctor Deepak Chopra argues that this type of medicine is based only on materialist presuppositions, focused on using medications or therapeutic practices only on the sick organ.

Biomedicine has little interest in the whole person and does not encourage particularly personal interactions between the patient and the caregiver. Such interactions might disturb scientific rationality and medical procedures, such as diagnostic investigations and analyses. Too close a relationship would risk subjectivity and prejudice the scientific rigour of prescriptions and the co-ordination of different kinds of specialized care. The

The discovery and pursuit of our mission gives us a reason to live, brings meaning to life, and builds self-esteem and self-confidence.

177

The spiritual question is at the heart of the preoccupation of modern holistic medicine.

sick are seen as objects of scientific study, with other aspects of their being systematically forgotten.

On the other hand, caregivers of the *healer* type exercise a transcendent function. They take into account all the aspects of the sick person: physical, emotional, social, and spiritual. They rely on their skills as they consider in particular the spiritual aspect of the patient.

The spiritual question is at the heart of the preoccupation of modern holistic medicine. Carl Jung believed that spirituality was an essential element for human psychic health; in all his patients who suffered from neuroses, he saw "the suffering of a soul that has lost its bearings."[58]

The healer recognizes the Self of the sick person and collaborates with it. The healer counts on the sick person's "inner healer," confident that this person possesses in himself or herself all the necessary resources for re-establishing health. In short, the healer stimulates the healing Self of the sick person so that the sick person can learn to heal himself or herself.

The wounded healer

Wounded healers possess particular wisdom. Their knowledge has been acquired through an initiation in which they experienced their own sickness and vulnerability, and healed themselves.

Unlike health-care professionals who rely only on their skills, wounded healers enable the sick person to learn from their experience of illness and healing.

They know the conditions on which healing depends: their experience of illness has left them humble and compassionate towards people who suffer. They always remember their own healed wounds, and their own vulnerability. They have gone beyond the fear of their illness returning, and even beyond anxiety in the face of death. We can thus say that they have partially integrated their shadow as healer: the fear of becoming sick themselves; the pleasure at seeing others stricken by illness; and the hope of social gain, as their remuneration and social standing come from the health problems of others. Unambiguously, wounded healers want the other person to be healed.

Healers know the emotional state of sick people and their inner turmoil; they sense the personal and social conflicts that led to the illness. They help the sick resolve conflicts by teaching them to forgive themselves and others. They motivate those who are sick to awaken their own healing power and to appreciate their progress, however small it might be, towards health.

I believe that sickness is brought on by inner conflict, a conflict between two parts of the self.

Sickness has psychological origins

When the conscience is fragmented,
it wages war
in the body-spirit system.

— DEEPAK CHOPRA

I believe that sickness is brought on by inner conflict, a conflict between two parts of the self: two opposing emotions (loving and hating a person); two clashing values (spending money on oneself or giving it to the poor); two attitudes (rebelling against the boss or obeying him blindly); two options (changing jobs or staying in the same job); two ethical obligations (being faithful to one's spouse or having a lover); two reactions (desiring vengeance or punishing ourselves); and so on.

Inner conflicts are aggravated by unhappy circumstances, such as the loss of someone close to us, a great disappointment, an insult that hurts us, the loss of reputation, the breakup of a friendship. In particular, when we are grieving, there is tension between controlling our emotions and needing to express them.

Inner conflict is a source of stress.

In the process of forgiveness, we are torn between the desires for vengeance and for self-blame by identifying with the offender. All of life's dramas contribute to a fragmentation of being in which the fragments clash with each other and destroy psychological balance. Often, physical illness follows such painful events. It is strange that the link between sickness and traumatic situations is made so rarely.

Inner conflict is a source of stress. Studies on stress tend to give importance to external factors while overlooking inner conflicts. When the tension between these inner stressors increases in intensity, it produces debilitating stress: distress. Among other things, distress weakens the immune system and makes the organism vulnerable to all manner of viruses and germs and, eventually, to all kinds of illnesses. The eminent researcher Hans Selye produced well-documented work on the dangers of too much stress.[59] Along the same lines, Dr. Ryke Geerd affirmed that he had discovered in the neurons of the brain actual traces of a psychological conflict turned biological. He explains that several types of cancer are due to unresolved psychological conflicts that are exacerbated by stressful situations.[60]

The sick person's situation is complicated when the conflict is partially unconscious. If a conscious part is provoking unconscious resistance, the sick person does not perceive the conflict or impasse in which he or she is living, but feels it as disease, anguish or anxiety. For example, many people want to get well, but unconsciously don't want to give up the advantages that being sick offers: rest, removal of responsibilities, a pretext for not feeling guilty, learned helplessness, and so on.

The Self as the inner healer

If the harmonizing action of the Self does not resolve it, the inner conflict tends to have repercussions on the body as disease. But if the Self manages to resolve the stressful polarization, the illness will disappear on its own, since no stress is fuelling it. This is what Carl Jung calls *reconciliatio oppositorum*, the reconciliation of opposites.

The recommended method for achieving this reconciliation is as follows. First, the healer must uncover in his client the stressful polarities that are manifested externally by simultaneous incongruity (for example, he shakes his head "No" and says "Yes") or a sequential incongruity (for example, he repeats "Yes, but…"). Second, the healer needs to intentionally situate the two poles of the polarity by anchoring them in each of the client's two hands. Third, by appealing to the client's Self, the healer asks him or her to integrate these two opposing parts. Finally, the healer offers suggestions for continuing the integration. Often, integrating symbols appear at this moment. They indicate the healing of these inner conflicts, as the opposing parts become complementary, constructive aspects of the personality.

This same phenomenon of integration happens in the world of artistic expression. Sometimes a work of art hits us, speaks to us, inspires us, makes us feel that an inner tension or conflict has reached a new level of resolution or integration.

CONCLUSION

I could have chosen archetypes other than the good father or mother, the sage, the guide, and the healer. But in these archetypes I see the greatest realization of happiness. Being loved and loving others, seeing our life through eyes of wisdom, finding our place in the Universe through pursuing our mission, and being able to heal ourselves are essential as we build lives of true happiness.

Being loved and loving others, seeing our life through eyes of wisdom, finding our place in the Universe through pursuing our mission, and being able to heal ourselves are essential as we build lives of true happiness.

Part III

From the spirituality of the Self
to Christian faith

CHAPTER 15

From the spirituality of the Self to Christian faith

A wisdom tradition or a religion that does not help human beings
to find their fulfillment [...] in daily life
risks becoming alienation.

— Bernard Hugueux

SOME CHRISTIAN SPIRITUALITIES
REJECT ESTEEMING THE SELF

Some Christian spiritualities are still burdened by the weight of past suspicions about self-esteem. They are afraid it will promote selfishness, the enemy of selfless love. In such a context, self-esteem seems like arrogance, and self-affirmation seems like pride. This was the most feared sin, that of Lucifer and rebellious heretics.

Supported by a Dolorist theology (a theology that preached the moral value or usefulness of suffering), this spirituality advocated disordered self-abasement and seeking humiliation. It offered to Christians a path of perfection on which we were supposed to find joy in being humiliated. It proposed the imitation of Christ who preferred the humiliation of the cross to the glory of the heavenly kingdom.

Maurice Bellet caricatures this spiritual orientation and denounces this supposedly Christian virtue that is fuelled by low self-esteem:

> Thus we should pay close attention to the esteem that we have for ourselves and the pretentiousness that results from it. We should focus on our liabilities rather than on the gifts we presume to have. We should fear success that goes to our head. We should prefer invisible, modest, contemptible work; it is scarcely worthy of the capabilities we think we have.

Some Christian spiritualities are still burdened by the weight of past suspicions about self-esteem.

Some kinds of contemporary spiritual literature preserve a sense of discomfort or uneasiness with regard to teachings about self-esteem as a source of the fulfillment of our being.

We should thank God for our failures: saving ordeals that bring us back to our true misery. [...] Thus we will be able to put into practice this self-hatred that the gospel recommends.[61]

This text reminds us of *The Imitation of Christ* and *The Degrees of Humility According to the Rule of St. Benedict*.[62] This vision of the person deformed the spirituality of thousands of religious educators, who in turn handed on this sad heritage to countless Christians.

People say to me, "That's all in the past. The younger generation doesn't think that way anymore." I'm not so sure. The movement of self-hatred still drives some Jansenist Christians who denounce, for instance, the contributions of the human sciences to the development of the person. Sebastian Moore laments the beliefs of these fundamentalist Christians. For him, setting Christian spirituality against a psychology that promotes self-esteem constitutes a terrible mistake. In fact, the poor self-image preached by this type of spirituality accentuates the effects of original sin instead of the transforming action of the Spirit.[63]

Some kinds of contemporary spiritual literature preserve a sense of discomfort or uneasiness with regard to teachings about self-esteem as a source of the fulfillment of our being. Here is a recent example. Bernard Pitaud, of the Institute of formation for clergy educators in Paris, states, "One thing is sure: for Christians, harmony with oneself is not an end in itself, and psychological healing is not salvation." He adds, "The summit of spiritual life is harmony, or rather, union with, God."[64] He juxtaposes "harmony with oneself" and "union with God," as though it would be preferable to reach harmony with God without at the same time looking for psychological balance. A few lines further in his article, he recognizes, however, that for most people union with God is unattainable because of their wounded emotions. He is therefore forced to admit, in spite of himself, that the path to union with God normally involves a psychological balance that comes from a healthy interiority, self-esteem, and the valuing of personal gifts, keeping in mind, of course, our sufferings.

In contemporary religious discourse we find serious efforts to enhance self-esteem and self-confidence.

While in contemporary religious discourse we find serious efforts to enhance self-esteem and self-confidence, the collective memory of Christian spirituality centred on humiliation still spans the generations and influences the behaviour of Christians. Some people continue to be haunted by it even as they rebel against it. They feel embarrassed by the formation in self-abasement and self-hatred that they received.

It's not surprising that psychologists, sociologists, and Freudian/Marxist/Nietzschean philosophers have gone in the exact opposite direction from this masochistic spirituality, and have lauded humanity's promethean grandeur and its all-powerful nature. These atheistic philosophies fall into the opposite extreme. They unduly glorify the human being while hiding human misery.

Such a deviant Christian spirituality confuses the virtue of Christian humility with humiliation. Humility, the honest recognition of our gifts and our limitations, has nothing to do with the sad search for humiliation. Furthermore, this train of thought perverts the mystery of the cross of Jesus Christ, making it a way of exalting pain. The passion of Jesus was a particular event, proof of enormous love for humanity. But it is not a model of suffering to be perpetuated. The resurrection, not the passion and death, comes first in God's thinking. Life has priority over death, and ultimately conquered it.

WITNESSES OF AUTHENTIC CHRISTIAN SPIRITUALITY POINT TO THE IMPORTANCE OF SELF-ESTEEM

During an interview in which he spoke of the self-esteem movement, the Swiss theologian Eric Fuchs remarked: "Not everything is negative in this search for fulfillment. Within expressions that are sometimes a bit baroque, there is something that sounds true to me: the willingness to live in harmony with oneself, to achieve this 'self-esteem' that Paul Ricoeur speaks about."[65] Here is a selection of quotes from Christian spiritual writers who, far from denigrating self-esteem, actually promote it.

First, some of the Fathers of the Church and the saints have expressed accurate views of the human being:

- "The glory of God is the human person fully alive, and the life of the human person is the vision of God." (Saint Irenaeus, second century)
- "No one is as close to you as you yourself." (Saint Bernard of Clairvaux, 1090)

Commenting on the passage from the gospel "You will love your neighbour as yourself" (Matthew 22.39), St. Thomas Aquinas, Doctor of the Church, writes

- "A man's love for himself is the model of his love for another."[66]

Now here are some testimonies from spiritual masters:

- "That I am human is what I have in common with other human beings. That I see and hear and eat and drink, that I do with all the animals. But that I am an 'I,' that belongs exclusively to me. This belongs to me alone, and to no one else, to no other human being, nor to the angels nor to God, except in the measure that I am one with him." (Meister Eckhart)

- "God's grandeur is revealed in human greatness." (20th-century spiritual writer Maurice Zundel)
- "Some people no longer love themselves and have lost the ability to love others. They retreat into a shell and advocate individualism. They must be reconciled with life." (Jean Vanier)[67]
- "How can a human being justly hate and deprecate in him- or herself what God has created in love? What God, what Father is there who would take pleasure in us disdaining, killing and finally destroying the image of God that we are?" (Maurice Bellet)
- "Devaluing people is an obstacle to making God credible, but a sense of the grandeur of the human person puts faith in God within reach." (English Benedictine monk Sebastian Moore)[68]

This approach to favouring self-esteem and esteeming the Self will have an important impact on those who preach the Christian gospel.

All these witnesses to Christian spirituality confirm that the fulfillment of the self, far from being an obstacle to Christian life is, in fact, its driving force. We draw on the capacity to love others and God in the capacity to love ourselves with a love that is neither capricious, selfish nor individualist.

This approach to favouring self-esteem and esteeming the Self will have an important impact on those who preach the Christian gospel.

It is essential that those who proclaim the Good News have high self-esteem. By their being and their actions, they should be "good news."

Jungian spirituality seeks out interiority and religious experience and invites us to see natural revelations of the divine in sacred symbols.

FROM THE SPIRITUALITY OF ESTEEMING THE SELF TO CHRISTIAN SPIRITUALITY

The passion for a spirituality of the Self

When I was giving a talk in Fribourg, Switzerland, a student asked, "Isn't it enough to have a spirituality of the Self, of the divine, rather than believing in all these religions?" The question suggests a firm distrust of institutionalized religions and an equal attraction for a natural spirituality, freed from all ecclesiastical constraints.

Similarly, it is interesting to consider the question "Is there a non-religious spirituality?"[69] Without getting into this debate, I will say that there is a relationship between the spirituality of the Self and a non-religious spirituality. Both are autonomous, sensitive to human dignity, searching for free thought, tolerant, mystical without being religious, a breath of life; they take up where religion leaves off and give an experience of the absolute.

While admitting these similarities, it is important to note that the Jungian spirituality of the Self does not reflect the politicized, anti-clerical spirituality called *secular*. Rather than being anti-religious, Jungian spirituality seeks out interiority and religious experience and invites us to see natural revelations of the divine in sacred symbols. It differs, however, from institutionalized religions with their dogmatic formulas and their set rituals. It is a psycho-spiritual process, a kind of wisdom; it opens a path to psychological maturity, at the heart of which lies the spiritual and the sacred. According to the spirituality of the Self, psycho-spiritual evolution has a goal: individuation. This term, used by Carl Jung, describes the most complete fulfillment of a person's being. Far from being anti-religious, the spirituality of the Self recognizes the primordial importance of religion, in the etymological sense of the word *religare*, "to join together." It is built on the divine character of the human soul and on transcendent archetypes that equally and naturally reveal the sacred.

Although Jung did not want to pass on a doctrinal tradition — "I can only hope and wish that no one becomes 'Jungian'" he once said — he has had successors who, through associations, have spread his discoveries and continued his research.

Jung's theories have given birth, among other things, to the humanist movement called "transpersonal," which M.A. Descamps describes in these terms: "A level of Being that transcends the individual ego or self, goes beyond the idea of the person in their states of non-ordinary expanded consciousness, and reaches the Self (Jung), the subconscious (Teilhard de Chardin), the Superhuman (Sri Aurobindo), the nature of Buddha [...] It is expressed by myths, symbols and peak experiences."[70]

In addition to these movements of natural spirituality, the analytical psychology of the Self gave rise to a loose conglomeration of different, eclectic spiritual movements that are all, for the most part, offspring of the New Age movement.

Briefly, the problems and opinions that the spirituality of the Self as conceived by Jung raises include the accusation of Gnosticism, the confusion of the notion of the Self and of God, the shadow side of God, and the possible excesses in the interpretation of symbols.

Let us now explore how the spirituality of the Self paves the way for Christian faith.

The analytical psychology of the Self gave rise to a loose conglomeration of different, eclectic spiritual movements.

The work on the self, and specifically the work on the Self offered by Jungian psychology, helps people discover and experience their souls.

THE SPIRITUALITY OF ESTEEMING THE SELF: ESSENTIAL FOR RECEPTIVITY TO CHRISTIAN FAITH

Affirming the human soul and its sacred character

In 1992, the theologian and Jungian psychotherapist John Sanford lamented the almost total absence of any concern for the human soul: "Today the idea of care of the soul has fallen by the wayside except in certain forms of mystical and introspective Christianity, and in certain psychologies, particularly, Jungian psychology."[71] Scarcely ten years later, the "care of the soul" has become a popular subject, not just among those who deal with spiritual issues, but also with psychologists who are more and more interested in the study of the Self. In an intriguing cycle, they have come back to the primary object of their science: the study of the human soul.

With the spirituality of the Self, Carl Jung went counter to all the atheistic humanisms of his time. He was not content to call the Self a central organizing principle of the personality, but qualified this Self as the *imago Dei*, the image of God. Thus he allied to his long scientific research the secular wisdom of the great religions. To name the soul, he borrowed from Buddhism the concept of the Self, and from Christianity, the image of God. In doing so, he affirmed that religions, in addition to binding the soul to God, are systems for healing psychological illnesses, and that psychology needs the insights, particularly of Buddhism and Christianity, to give it a wisdom that goes beyond psychology.[72]

The work on the self, and specifically the work on the Self offered by Jungian psychology, helps people discover and experience their souls. By diverse techniques and by strategies suggested by both the negative and positive paths, people not only keep in touch with their souls, they consider this contact as an essential factor in their healing and fulfillment. All these approaches to the care of the soul harmonize well with those of the Christian tradition, such as prayer, meditation, contemplation, and the use of symbols in sacramental rites.

The spirituality of the Self is built on desire for the infinite

The spirituality of the Self thus opens up onto spiritual and eternal realities expressed by universal and natural mythic themes.

The Self and its symbols evoke in us the desire for the infinite. Openness to the infinite takes the form of symbolic images of the Self that represent totality, the absolute, and the infinite, as we saw in Chapter 9 – such as the pearl of great price, the indestructible diamond, pure gold, living water, the rebirth of the phoenix from its ashes, the elixir of immortality, the philosopher's stone, and the kingdom. Then there are the figures that comprise the centre around which all space is organized: the mandala, the cross, the North star, and cubic and circular figures. The spirituality of the Self thus opens up onto spiritual and eternal realities expressed by universal and natural mythic themes. This spirituality moves its practitioners towards a spiritual awakening and a thirst for the infinite. In this way, it is preparation for the act of faith in God who alone can satisfy this desire for the infinite.

In terms of this human longing for the infinite, we can profit from reading Jean Houston's thoughts on the quest for the divine beloved.[73]

Without a strong spirituality, faith has a tendency to remain superficial and sociological.

Longing for the infinite: the foundation of the act of faith in Jesus Christ

Jesus: "Do you also wish to go away?"
Peter: "Lord, to whom can we go?
You have the words of eternal life."

— JOHN 6.68

Meditating on the great symbols created by the Self stirs up a immense appetite and desire for the fullness of life. A question then springs up spontaneously in our hearts: "Who or what can satisfy this huge longing?"

In response, the Christian faith names and personalizes the One who can fulfill these infinite longings of the human heart. Sebastian Moore believes this to be true. After raising the question of the relationship between spirituality and faith, he says, "Spirituality is almost indispensable to a living faith, but these are distinct realities [...] Faith is a free and personal response to the longings discovered through spirituality."[74] The passage from spirituality to faith "is the sudden feeling of a personal Presence whereas we were longing for something that seemed unknown to us."[75] Without a strong spirituality, faith has a tendency to remain superficial and sociological.

Moore then compares the forms of meditation practised in different spiritualities and Christian prayer. Meditation brings us close to mystery, but it does not allow us to enter into the mystery of a Person. Only by a special grace given through the mystery discovered in meditation does the image of a Person emerge. I have known a good many people who have felt suddenly called by God or Christ through interior revelations during sessions of transcendental, New Age or Christian meditation.

They moved from meditation to prayer. Prayer, which names the Person behind the mystery, places us in the realm of faith.

Often the journey to faith first leads us on a search for the Self or the infinite.

Often the journey to faith first leads us on a search for the Self or the infinite. The path of many converts begins with the experience of the soul. Raïssa Maritain, wife of the philosopher Jacques Maritain, had an experience of the Self that illustrates this process well: "Before I received the faith, a subtle intuition had often given me the experience of the reality of my being, of the profound first principle that came to me out of nothing. A powerful insight whose violence sometimes shocked me and which was the first to give me the knowledge of a metaphysical absolute."[76]

Her witness is echoed in a well-known passage from the Confessions of St. Augustine:

Late have I loved you, O Beauty ever ancient, ever new, late have I loved you! You were within me, but I was outside ... You were with me, but I was not with you.

The experience of the Self can qualify as natural mysticism: "A fruitful experience of the absolute," of the substantial reality of the soul that has been overcome, as Jacques Maritain says. He adds, "The word *absolute* is purposely written without a capital A. For as we will see later, not every mystical experience is an experience of God."[77]

The act of faith: a form of hope

As I said earlier, faith is not a purely intellectual endeavour, but a movement of the soul that identifies its longings for the infinite with the person of Jesus Christ. The act of faith is the acceptance of a person in whom we hope to find eternal life.

Thomas Aquinas cites the definition of the virtue of faith that St. Paul gives: "Now faith is the assurance of things hoped

This relationship between the symbolism of the Self and faith is clearly revealed in the sacrament of baptism.

for, the conviction of things not seen."[78] Faith is rooted in the hope of perfect happiness. Note that the desire for happiness springs from the Self, and that Jesus Christ comes to fulfill this desire.

A spirituality of the Self based only on the archetypes of the collective unconscious will never produce an act of Christian faith. It is by divine revelation that we respond, accepting the historical event of Jesus Christ and entering into communion with the Trinitarian God who is Father, Son, and Spirit. The spirituality of the Self helps us to discover the existence of the sacred and of the divine, and is thus a preamble to faith. The revelation by Jesus Christ of the divine nature, Father, Son, and Spirit, brings to fulfillment the revelation started by the Self.

Knowledge of the Self and faith, then, are not only *not* contradictory, they are complementary. Knowledge of the sacred world revealed by the Self calls for faith. Faith, properly understood, sustains the soul in its search for truth and sustains progress in caring for the soul, according to the maxim *fides quaerens intellectum* ("faith seeking understanding").

Faith and archetypes

This relationship between the symbolism of the Self and faith is clearly revealed in the sacrament of baptism. The newly baptized person has the archetypal experience of death and resurrection signified by being plunged into the water and, at the same time, makes an explicit act of faith in Jesus Christ. In a masterful article,[79] the theologian and anthropologist Louis Beirnaert writes that the archetypal experience lived in the baptismal ritual cannot on its own bring about the assent of faith.

The person about to be baptized must, with the help of grace, make a solemn decision and renounce the forces of evil and declare their adherence to Christ. However, Beirnaert adds that a conscious act of faith that is not nourished by a ritual – in the case of baptism, by immersion in and coming up out of the water – would lack depth. The unconscious would not be engaged in the act of faith. The baptismal ritual would unfold in a simplistic, superficial manner and would not convert the depths of the unconscious. Beirnaert adds that such a baptism would lack incarnation; the danger would be that the old demons of paganism would resurface.

At the end of his article, he makes the following recommendation: "It is not a question of theologians renouncing the assent of faith, but rather of exploring an aspect of religious symbolism that is too neglected and of accepting the help of mythologists and psychologists.[80]

The spirituality of self-esteem and esteeming the Self, far from denying Christian spirituality, opens the way for it and accompanies it.

The spirituality of self-esteem and esteeming the Self, far from denying Christian spirituality, opens the way for it and accompanies it.

CONCLUSION

Self-esteem, esteeming the Self, and Christian faith prove to be three complementary realities in the formation of the human being. While self-esteem is exalted in our society, which celebrates individual progress, esteeming the Self, the care of the soul, is neglected. This is why people today are clamouring for spirituality.

Despite the widespread hunger for things spiritual, some Christian spiritualities cut themselves off from developments in psychology, especially in terms of self-esteem, and thus become sterile and outdated. They no longer respond to the longings of the modern world.

If this same Christian spirituality becomes protective of its turf, and defends itself against the contributions of other

The care of the soul, the cultivation of the spirituality of the Self, is central to the growth of faith.

spiritualities, it quickly develops a tendency to cloister itself in a sectarian, institutional attitude. Faith needs the Self's structures of spiritual hospitality and its rich symbolism in order to gain access to the depths of the unconscious.

In my opinion, the care of the soul, the cultivation of the spirituality of the Self, is central to the growth of faith. The current challenge to psychology is to rediscover the soul and its expressions. This is the psychological movement – the humanistic and transpersonal movement – begun by Jung, Maslow, and Frankl.

In my view, there exists a clear continuity between self-esteem and esteeming the Self, and between self-esteem, esteeming the Self, and Christian faith.

Glossary

Acceptance of self

Knowing how to accept and integrate our gifts and faults so we will have a good self-image.

Active imagination

A method of assimilating unconscious material (dreams, fantasies, etc.) by forms of conscious expression (dialogue, artistic expressions, etc.).

Anima and *animus*

The contra-sexual shadow of a woman is the *animus*, her inner male whose qualities are repressed to allow feminine traits to emerge. The contra-sexual shadow of a man is called the *anima*, the inner woman whose qualities are pushed back into the unconscious to allow masculine traits to emerge.

Archetypes

Forms of energy that constitute the primordial and structural elements of the psyche. When archetypes express themselves in images or symbols, this reality is called an *archetypal image*.

Conscious "I"

Synonymous with the ego, the conscious self also means the self with a small "s". It is a psychological centre of feelings, emotions, sensations, words, beliefs, needs, desires, of will, fantasies, thoughts, etc. The "I" has been compared to a projector that shines its light over the vast expanse of consciousness, highlighting these different aspects of consciousness.

The conscious "I" depends on the Self, of which it is a distant reflection, for its formation. In self-esteem, the "I" is equivalent to the "self."

Ego

The Latin term designating the conscious "I" or the conscious self. Sometimes it takes on the sense of a social self or an ideal self in some popular expressions, such as "an inordinately large ego or an overblown ego."

Ideal self

See persona.

Individuation

Process of psychic differentiation designed to promote the autonomy of the individual. It is the progressive liberation from all undue external influences to guarantee the individual's freedom. Individuation is the goal of all human growth.

Love of self

Showing compassion and kindness towards oneself.

Persona (ideal self)

The persona, in its etymological sense (of *per* and *sonna*) represents the mask that actors wore to reveal their role in a play and to project their voices. On a psychological level, the word *persona* signifies the faculty of adapting to the expectations of the surrounding community and culture of a milieu.

When it becomes too heavy and constraining for the individual, the persona is often assimilated to a social superego. In psychological literature, it is designated by the expression "ideal self."

Psyche

The sum of conscious and unconscious psychological and spiritual processes.

Religiosity

All natural spiritual activity or natural wisdom. The Self, the person's deep identity, is by nature religious and sacred, because it links the diverse components of the human psyche. The word *religion* is used here in its etymological sense (from *religare*, the action of making links between various realities).

Revealed religions

Refers to the activities of the prophets who called themselves bearers of a message that came from a divinity. They rely on the natural revelation (archetypes) common to the Self, but often take the form of social and cultural institutions.

Self

The highest psychic authority at the heart of a person. Naturally abstract, the Self (with a capital "S") constitutes the deep spiritual identity of every human being. It imposes a subtle direction on the self. It is the "soul inhabited by the divine," (the *imago Dei*), according to Jung's beautiful expression.

It constitutes the central archetype of human beings; it is represented by the centre of energy of the mandala that reconciles the opposing traits of psychic realities. It is the organizing principle of the whole personality; it has no gender, since it is a synthesis of masculine and feminine traits. It is eternal; it does not die and is always young. Therefore it is a healing principle. It has the power to harmonize the psychic fragmentation caused by wounds and, consequently, to reduce bodily stress. Moreover, because it is in relationship with the Universe, it puts the person in contact with the cosmic forces of creation.

Self-affirmation

Affirmation is linked to the self-presentation of a person and their competence. It requires specific skills in expressing self-esteem which, additionally, are the fruit of an inner life. Synonymous with being sure of one's self (the opposite of doubting oneself), believing in oneself.

Self-confidence

This expression designates those aspects of self-esteem that deal with action and competence. Having confidence in oneself is believing in one's capacities to learn, to make judgments and anticipate success. Synonyms: self-assurance, self-satisfaction, pride in oneself, having faith in one's endeavours.

Self-esteem

Assessment that persons give themselves as much for their person as for their abilities. For a negative assessment of the self (both for the person and their competence), the term *low self-esteem* is used.

Self-esteem has different components, both positive and negative: people speak of love of self and the gift of self, acceptance and lack of acceptance of the self, of valuing the self and putting oneself down.

Formerly used in a pejorative sense, this word signified "arrogance" and "self-importance." It has been brought back into favour.

Self-love

See self-esteem.

Shadow

The unconscious complex that consists of the uneducated or repressed part of the self. It is formed by the fear of rejection by important people in our circle. Unconscious, it needs to be harmonized with the conscious qualities of the self in order to build solid self-esteem.

Strong self (high self-esteem)

The strong self is the same as a conscious, autonomous "I" that is disengaged both from the external expectations that are unintegrated by the self (persona) and from the shadow, whose qualities it has integrated.

Synchronicity

A phenomenon in which an external event coincides in a significant way with a psychological state of the spirit.

Transcendental function of the Self

According to Jung, the path of growth for an individual passes through the dialogue of the conscious self with the Self by the intermediary of symbolic messages coming from the unconscious (dreams, fantasies, peak experiences, etc.). He calls this process "the transcendental function" that happens unexpectedly in the tension between the conscious and the unconscious and promotes the union of the two.

Weak self (low self-esteem)

A conscious "I" both partially constrained by the expectations of others (persona) and weakened by the constant struggle with the complexes of the shadow.

Notes

1   N. Branden, *The Six Pillars of Self-Esteem* (New York: Bantam Books, 1994).

2   Branden, 4.

3   Branden, 27.

4   S. Coopersmith, *The Antecedents of Self-Esteem* (Mountain View, CA: Consulting Psychologists Press, Inc., 1981).

5   B. Coloroso, *Winning at Parenting... Without Beating Your Kids* (Littleton, CO: Kids Are Worth It, Inc., 1989), 2 cassettes.

6   St. Thomas Aquinas, *Summa theologica* IIa, Q.26, art.4.

7   To read more about this process, see J. Monbourquette, *How to Forgive: A Step-by-Step Guide* (Ottawa: Novalis, 2000).

8   D. W. Winnicott, *Maturational Processes and the Facilitating Environment: Studies in the Theory of Emotional Development* (International Universities Press, June 1965).

9   According to P. Coelho, *The Alchemist*, trans. Alan R. Clarke (San Francisco: HarperSanFrancisco, 1993), xiii.

10 For more on the shadow, see J. Monbourquette, *How to Befriend Your Shadow: Welcoming Your Unloved Side* (Ottawa: Novalis, 2001).

11 M. Lacroix, "Le développement personnel: Un nouveau culte du moi," *Christus : Revue de formation spirituelle*, ["Personal development: a new cult of the self"; *Christus: A Journal of Spiritual Formation*] t. 47, no 188, octobre 2000, 406.

12 Lacroix, 406.

13 D. Richo, *Shadow Dance: Liberating the Power and Creativity of Your Dark Side* (Boston: Shambhala, 1999), 94.

14 C.G. Jung and R. Cahen, *Racines de la conscience: Études sur l'archétype, sous la direction de R. Cahen.* [Roots of consciousness: Studies about the archetype, directed by R. Cahen.] (Paris: Buchet-Chastel, 1971), 280.

15 R. A. Johnson, *Owning Your Own Shadow: Understanding the Dark Side of the Psyche* (San Francisco: HarperSanFrancisco, 1991), 82.

16 Quoted in J. Firman, *Je et Soi: Nouvelles perspectives en psychosynthèse* [I and Self: Revisioning Psychosythesis] (Sainte Foy, QC: Centre d'intégration de la personne de Québec, 1992), 271.

17 É. G. Humbert, *L'homme aux prises avec l'inconscient* [Man struggling with the unconscious] (Paris: Albin Michel, 1992), 65.

18 C. G. Jung, *New Paths in Psychology, Collected Works: Psychology and Religion: West and East* (Princeton University Press, 1938), 399.

19 E. C. Whitmont, *The Symbolic Quest: Basic Concepts of Analytical Psychology* (Princeton, NJ: Princeton University Press, 1991), 218-219.

20 Firman, 312.

21 S. Gilligan, *Self-Relations Psychotherapy: Demonstrating the Principles and Practices of Self-Relations Psychotherapy* (VHS) (Encinitas, CA: n.d.).

22 Whitmont, 217.

23 Firman, 184.

24 C. J. Jung, *Mysterium conjunctionis: Études sur la separation et la reunion des opposes psychiques dans l'alchimie*, avec la coll. De M.-L. von Franz, [*Mysterium conjunctionis*: Studies on the separation and reunion of psychic opposites in alchemy, with the collaboration of M.-L. von Franz] volume I (Paris: Albin Michel, 1980), 153.

25 Jung and Cahen, *Racines de la conscience*, 553.

26 Whitmont, 219.

27 Whitmont, 222.

28 Cited by Y. Tardan-Mascquelier, *Jung, la sacralité de l'expérience intérieure* [Jung, the sacredness of the inner experience] (Paris: Droguet et Ardant, 1992), 222-223.

29 Jung, *Mysterium conjunctionis*, 168.

30 See J. Monbourquette, *How to Befriend Your Shadow: Welcoming Your Unloved Side* (Ottawa: Novalis, 2001), 117-121.

31 C. G. Jung, *Dialectique du moi et de l'inconscient* [The dialectic of the self and the unconscious] (Paris: Gallimard, 1964), 111.

32 A. de Lamartine (1790–1869), Milly ou la terre natale (I).

33 C. G. Jung, *"Ma vie": souvenirs, rêves et pensées,* ("My Life": memories, dreams, reflections), collected and published by A. Jaffé (Paris: Gallimard, 1966), 263.

34 Whitmont, 217.

35 H. Le Saux, *Éveil à Soi, éveil à Dieu: Essai sur la prière* [Awakening to the Self, awakening to God: Essay on Prayer] (Paris: Oeil, 1986).

36 Quoted in Y. Tardan-Masquelier, "Maximes de vie," *Actualité des Religions,* no. 36, March 2002, 25.

37 A. H. Maslow, *Towards a Psychology of Being* (Toronto: D. Van Nostrand Co., 1968), 71.

38 Maslow, 71.

39 D. Hay and K. Hunt, "Is Britain's Soul Waking Up?" *The Tablet,* June 24, 2000, 846.

40 M.-L. von Franz, *On Dreams and Death: A Jungian Interpretation* (Boston: Shambhala, 1987), 24-40.

41 S. Mongeau, *La simplicitee volontaire, plus que jamais* [Voluntary simplicity, more than ever] revised and enlarged edition (Montreal: Éditions Écosociété, 1998).

42 C. Andreas and T. Andreas, *Core Transformation: Reaching the Wellspring Within* (Moab, UT: The Real People Press, 1994), 19.

43 J. Monbourquette, *How to Love Again: Moving from Grief to Growth* (Ottawa: Novalis, 2001), 48.

44 R. Bly, *The Little Book on the Human Shadow* (New York: William Booth, 1988), 15.

45 C. G. Jung, *New Paths in Psychology,* 528.

46 S. Naifeh, "Archetypal Foundations of Addiction and Recovery," *Journal of Analytical Psychology*, vol. 40, no. 2, April 1995, 148.

47 M-L. von Franz, *Reflets de l'âme: Les projections, recherché de l'unité intérieur dans la psychologie do C.G. Jung* [Reflections of the Soul: Projections from inner unity in psychology] (Orsay: Editions Entrelacs, 1992), 15.

48 C. G. Jung, *Modern Man in Search of a Soul* (New York: Harvest Books, 1933).

49 Quoted in S. F. Fincher, *La voie du mandala* [The way of the mandala] (St.-Jean-de-Braye: Éditions Dangles, 1996), 16.

50 To those who want to follow up on a process of meditation on mandalas, I suggest the manual *Mandalas of the World: A Meditating and Painting Guide* by R. Dahlike (New York: Sterling Publishing, 2004). For those who want to begin drawing mandalas, I recommend J. Cornell's *Mandala: Luminous Symbols for Healing* (Wheaton, IL: Quest Books, 1994).

51 J. Houston, *The Search for the Beloved: Journeys in Sacred Psychology* (Los Angeles: Jeremy P. Tarcher, 1987), 92.

52 R. Metzner, *Opening to the Light: Ways of Human Transformation* (Los Angeles: Jeremy P. Tarcher, 1986), vi-viii.

53 Firman, 290.

54 "Forgiveness and Self-Respect" in *The World of Forgiveness*, vol. 1, no. 2. See the website of the International Institute of Forgiveness (*www.forgiveness-institute.org*).

55 Jung, *Modern Man in Search of a Soul.*

56 V. Frankl, *Découvrir un sens à sa vie: Avec la logothérapie* [Man's Search for Meaning: An Introduction to Logotherapy] (Montreal: Éditions de l'Homme, 1988), 199-120.

57 Firman, 190.

58 Jung, *Modern Man in Search of a Soul.*

59 H. Selye, *Stress Without Distress* (Hagerstown, MD: Lippincott Williams & Wilkins, 1974).

60 See his website: www.medecinenouvelle.com

61 M. Bellet, "De la nécéssité de s'éstimer soi-même," [On the necessity of self-esteem] *Christus: Revue de formation spirituelle*, no. 104, t. 26, October 1979, 390-391.

62 Examples given by A. Christophe and F. Lelord in their book *L'éstime de soi* [Self-esteem], 37.

63 S. Moore, *Let This Mind Be in You: The Quest for Identity Through Oedipus to Christ* (Minneapolis, MN: Winston Press, 1985), 47.

64 B. Pitaud, "Perdre sa vie pour la trouver" [Lose our life to find it], *Christus: Revue de formation spirituelle*, Vol. 47, no. 188, October 2000, 429.

65 J.-P. Guetry. "S'estimer soi-même. Une interview d'Eric Fuchs" ["Self-esteem: an interview with Eric Fuchs], *L'Actualité religieuse*, no. 168, July-August 15, 1998, 34.

66 *Summa theologica*, IIa, Q.26, art.4.

67 Jean Vanier, speaking at a conference at Notre Dame Cathedral in Ottawa, May 18, 1998.

68 Thanks to my friend Gérald Crausaz, who provided me with most of the texts quoted here.

69 *Actualité des Religions* no. 27, May 2001, 12-15.

70 Quoted by Y. Tardan-Masquelier in *Jung, la sacralité de l'expérience intérieur* [Jung, the sacredness of inner experience], 204.

71 J. A. Sanford, *Healing Body and Soul: The Meaning of Illness in the New Testament and Psychotherapy* (Louisville, KY: Westminster/John Knox, 1992), 58.

72 C.G. Jung, *Modern Man in Search of a Soul* (New York: Harcourt, Brace & World, 1969), 240-241.

73 Houston, 122-145.

74 Moore, 40.

75 Moore, 40.

76 Quoted by L. Gardet and O. Lacombe in *L'expérience du Soi : Étude de mystique comparée* [The experience of the Self: A comparative study of mystics] (Paris: Desclée De Brouwer, 1981), 34.

77 Gardet and Lacombe, 23.

78 *Summa theologica* IIa, Q.4, art.I.

79 L. Beirnaert, "Symbolism mythique de l'eau dans le baptême" [The mythical symbolism of water in baptism], *La maison-Dieu: Revue de Pastorale Liturgique* (Paris, Éditions du Cerf, no. 22, 2nd trimester 1950), 94-120.

80 Beirnaert, 120.

John Monbourquette is a psychotherapist, best-selling author and Catholic priest. While he has both taught high school and worked as a parish priest, his principal interest has been in the relationship between spirituality and psychology. His graduate studies in theology and psychology, and his doctoral studies in psychology at the International College of Los Angeles, have enabled him to pursue these interests both in the academic world, where he was a professor in the pastoral institute of Saint Paul University, Ottawa, and in his own private practice as a psychologist. His special areas of interest include forgiveness, self-esteem, male violence, the dynamics of grief, and accompanying the dying.

He has given hundreds of conferences on these topics in Canada and Europe to both professional and lay audiences. He is the author of *How to Forgive: A Step-by-Step Guide*; *How to Discover Your Personal Mission*; *How to Love Again: Moving from Grief to Growth*; and *How to Befriend Your Shadow: Welcoming Your Unloved Side* (all published by Novalis).

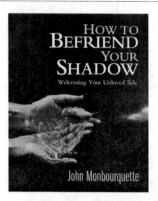

How to Befriend Your Shadow
Welcoming Your Unloved Side

Each of us has a "shadow," composed of everything we have driven back into our unconscious for fear of being rejected by the people we loved when we were young. Over the years, we created a whole underground world filled with things that were shameful, displeasing or upsetting to those around us.

Our task as adults is to rediscover what makes up our shadow, to bring it into the light, and to use it for our own spiritual growth. If we refuse to do this work, we risk being out of balance psychologically, and our lives and relationships will not reach their fullest potential.

Is your shadow your friend or your enemy? That will depend on how you see it and how you relate to it. This book offers you the tools you need to welcome your shadow side. Befriend your shadow, and watch your relationship with yourself and with others grow and deepen!

- 160 pages
- paperback
- ISBN 2-89507-082-2

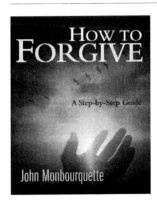

How to Forgive
A Step-by-Step Guide

This unique resource offers profound and practical advice on overcoming the emotional, spiritual, and psychological blocks to true forgiveness.

John Monbourquette begins by exploring the nature of forgiveness and exploding some of the myths. He shows how essential forgiveness is for us all, whatever our beliefs, for forgiveness touches on all aspects of the human person: the biological and psychological as well as the spiritual. He then takes the reader through his twelve-step healing process, providing practical exercises, case histories, anecdotes, and even poetry along the way.

How to Forgive is an honest and touching book that unlocks the liberating and transformative power of forgiveness.

- 198 pages
- paperback
- ISBN 2-89507-022-9

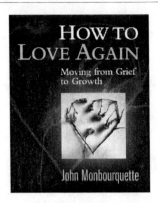

How to Love Again
Moving from Grief to Growth

Are you suffering from a deep loss in your life? *How to Love Again** is a book that can offer you comfort in a time of despair. It is intended to accompany you on the journey you are about to make. You may want to read it from cover to cover, meditate on it, or refer back to those passages that most inspire you.

John Monbourquette describes the kind of healing that comes after loss: "In the same way the physical body deals with a physical wound, the emotional body begins a healing process the moment the emotional trauma occurs. Allow the natural wisdom of your healing system to come to your rescue. Eventually the pain will subside, and you will then be more aware of life around you, more open to happiness, more fully human once again. In this way, you will move from grief to growth, and learn how to love again."

- 168 pages
- paperback
- ISBN 2-89507-180-2

* Revised edition, previously published as *To Love Again: Finding Comfort and Meaning in Times of Grief.*

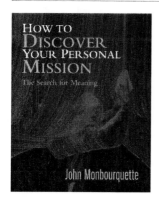

How to Discover Your Personal Mission
The Search for Meaning

What is your personal mission in life? Many of us find it hard to answer this question. It is so easy to get caught up in the day-to-day concerns of paying the rent and putting food on the table that we lose sight of the bigger picture. Whether we are young or not so young, we may feel that we haven't quite found our mission, that we're not doing what we feel we should be doing.

This user-friendly book invites you on an adventure to discover your personal mission. John Monbourquette will lead you through a three-stage process: learning to let go of the past; deepening your sense of identity and mission; and risking a new beginning in life. Through exercises and reflection, you will find the path that leads you in the direction that your soul is calling you.

Let the journey begin…

- 198 pages
- paperback
- ISBN 2-89507-163-2

Books by John Monbourquette are available
from your local bookstore or from Novalis
1-800-387-7164
www.novalis.ca

NOVALIS